THE JUNIOR ASTROLOGER'S HANDBOOK

A Kid's Guide to Astrological Signs, the Zodiac, and More

NIKKI VAN DE CAR

Illustrations by **UTA KROGMANN**

RP|KIDS

PHILADELPHIA

Running Press Kids
Hachette Book Group
1290 Avenue of the Americas, New York, NY 10104
www.runningpress.com/rpkids
@RP_kids

Printed in China

First Edition: July 2021

Published by Running Press Kids, an imprint of Perseus Books, LLC,
a subsidiary of Hachette Book Group, Inc. The Running Press Kids name and logo
is a trademark of the Hachette Book Group.

The Hachette Speakers Bureau provides a wide range of authors for speaking events.
To find out more, go to www.hachettespeakersbureau.com or call (866) 376-6591.

The publisher is not responsible for websites (or their content)
that are not owned by the publisher.

Print book cover and interior design by Frances J. Soo Ping Chow.

Library of Congress Cataloging-in-Publication Data
Names: Van De Car, Nikki, author. | Krogmann, Uta, illustrator.
Title: The junior astrologer's handbook : a kid's guide to astrological signs,
the zodiac, and more / Nikki Van De Car ; illustrations by Uta Krogmann.
Identifiers: LCCN 2020045584 | ISBN 9780762499557 (hardback) |
ISBN 9780762499540 (ebook)
Subjects: LCSH: Astrology--Juvenile literature.
Classification: LCC BF1708.1 .V345 2021 | DDC 133.5--dc23
LC record available at https://lccn.loc.gov/2020045584

ISBNs: 978-0-7624-9955-7 (hardcover), 978-0-7624-9954-0 (ebook)

APS

10 9 8 7 6 5 4 3 2 1

CONTENTS

INTRODUCTION

You know how you just *know* when someone is supposed to be your friend? You see them in a new class, at the park, or even just walking down the street, and you think, "We would get each other."

Maybe there's a reason for that. Maybe you were *meant* to be friends. Maybe it was written in the stars.

The theory of astrology is that the movements of celestial bodies—like the planets and certain constellations—reflect what is happening to us here on earth. So we can use the movements of the stars to help us understand what's going on in our lives—and help us get to know ourselves better.

You probably know your sign of the zodiac that is based on the day and month you were born and maybe what type of personality a person with that sign is supposed to have. But what else do you know about astrology?

The zodiac includes and takes its names from twelve constellations that arc across the sky; these are the constellations that the planets appear to move through from our perspective on earth as the earth travels around the sun. Each of those constellations has certain characteristics that can give you insight into your personality. So if you're a Virgo, you're probably a little bit shy, because most Virgos are. But that's not all. Within each sign are different divisions, called decans, which are sort of like subpersonalities that highlight certain aspects of the overall sign. So if you've found that you've never *really* felt like you fit the characteristics of the sign you supposedly are—for instance, you're a Leo but you're not nearly the drama queen Leos are supposed to be—that may be explained by the decan you fall into. The first decan is the classic version of what your sign is supposed to be, and it falls in the first third of the month. The second and third decans fall in the second and third parts of the month—obviously—and they can be just a little different because they are affected by different planets moving into your sign.

The signs also fall into the elemental categories of fire, water, earth, and air. The Fire Signs are Aries, Leo, and Sagittarius. The Water Signs are Cancer, Scorpio, and Pisces. The Earth Signs are Taurus, Virgo, and Capricorn, and the Air Signs are Aquarius, Gemini, and Libra. Although each sign has its own personality traits, it will also have many traits in common with other signs of its element—and because we like hanging out with people we have a lot in common with, Water Signs tend to be friends with each other, and Fire Signs with each other, and so on. On the other hand, opposites attract, so if someone is going to be your very best friend, then you'll want someone who balances you, who is calm when you are fiery, patient when you are frustrated.

The first half of this book will jump right in and offer general guidelines for life situations, like dealing with schoolwork, friends, and family, based on the signs of the zodiac. Through meditations and quizzes, you'll be able to use the information you have about your sign to figure out some dos and don'ts.

The back half of the book goes into more detail about each sign. The signs are usually organized according to the seasons, rather than the calendar year, so they will be listed here starting with Aries in the spring. There's a lot of information here, including more specifics about the decans and elemental connections. You can use this section to look deeper at the qualities or your own sign—and those of your family and friends—or as a reference to help you gain a deeper understanding of the day-to-day advice given in the first half.

At its core, astrology is not a rulebook. It doesn't tell you how you *have to* act—you may not necessarily be as impatient as your typical Sagittarius, and you may be way more chill than most Aries are. But when things feel fuzzy, when you're not sure who is your friend and who isn't or what you should be focusing on in school, or why suddenly everything seems to be going wrong, astrology is a tool you can use to help you figure things out.

PART I

What Signs Are You?
Sun Sign, Moon Sign, Rising Sign

If you're reading this book, you're probably already into astrology at least a little bit, so you know the first sign everyone learns about based on the day you were born: your Sun Sign. So if you were born between July 23 and August 22, the sun was in Leo, so you're a Leo, and so on for the other signs. And that sign says a lot about you—but it's not the whole picture. If you've never really identified with your sign, there's a good reason for that.

There are two *other* signs that play a major part in understanding your identity you may not have heard about. Your Moon Sign relates to where the moon was at the time you were born, and your Rising Sign relates to which new sign was creeping up over the horizon when you came into this world.

This isn't something most of us know offhand, but you can check online to find out what they are. Search for "What is my Moon Sign?" and "What is my Rising Sign?" and enter in your birth date and time. If you don't know what time you were born, it is included on your birth certificate or you can ask your parents.

These three signs together make up who we are as people. They interact with each other, contradict each other, and enhance each other. Roughly, your Sun Sign makes up the core of who you truly are, while your Moon Sign is your inner, emotional self, and your Rising Sign is the face you show to the outside world. If you're a Leo with a Pisces Moon Sign and a Sagittarius Rising Sign, then you are superfiery, and everyone sees you that way. But sometimes, deep down, you don't *feel* that way.

It's important to look at all three signs together in order to really understand astrology and how to use it. Your Sun Sign is the simplest, but it's not the whole story—and so it's not the whole *you*. If your Sun Sign is complemented by opposing forces in your Moon and Rising Signs, then you might want to look to one of them, or to a combination of the three, in order to understand yourself. Use the following quiz to determine which of your signs is most aligned with your core identity. Take the quiz for your Sun Sign to start. Then follow with your Moon and Rising Signs. And just see what feels right. Then, as you go through this book, work with the sign or combination of signs that feels truest to you. You know yourself best!

QUIZ

ARE YOU A TRUE _____?

H ere's how to take this quiz: First, find your Sun Sign, and test yourself with the list of statements about that sign. How often do the statements about this sign line up with your actions? Is this really you? Add up the number for your response to each statement to get your score and find out. If not, move on to your Rising Sign. Find it in the same list and try out the statements for that sign. Are these more like it? Then if need be, look at your Moon Sign. (If you try out your different signs, the higher the number, the better the match.) Don't worry: you'll find yourself!

1 = Never   2 = Hardly ever   3 = Sometimes
4 = Most of the time   5 = Always

ARIES

• I'm usually at the front lines of whatever is cool and fashionable.

• I like to be in charge.

• I don't back down from a fight—in fact, I usually win.

• I'm always looking for something fun and exciting to do.

• I look great in red.

If you got 16 or more, you're probably a true Aries.

TAURUS

• I love beautiful things.

• My friends know that I will never let them down.

• I don't give up on something until I've finished it.

• I'm really protective of those that I care about.

• It's frustrating when people don't understand that I'm right.

If you got 16 or more, you're probably a true Taurus.

GEMINI

• I'm great at communicating.

• Sometimes I want to be social . . . but other times
I just want to be alone.

• I think the world is just an incredible place.

• Sometimes I'm confused by my own emotions.

• I really like having someone to talk to.

If you got 16 or more, you're probably a true Gemini.

CANCER

• I am extremely loyal and empathetic.

• I care so much about my family.

• I can be a little moody at times.

• I can rely on my intuition—it hardly ever
leads me astray.

• I love helping those I care about.

If you got 16 or more, you're probably a true Cancer.

LEO

• I can pretty much always get people to like me.

• I am supercreative.

• I can be a little dramatic sometimes.

• I'm warmhearted and generous.

• I hate being ignored.

If you got 16 or more, you're probably a true Leo.

VIRGO

• I can be a little shy.

• I love animals and nature.

• I pay close attention to detail.

- I hate when people are rude.

- I'm pretty practical.

If you got 16 or more, you're probably a true Virgo.

LIBRA

- I work well with others.

- It's important that everything is fair and equal.

- I really don't like it when I'm forced to choose a side.

- I love it when everyone is getting along.

- I love hanging out with my friends; I don't like to be alone.

If you got 16 or more, you're probably a true Libra.

SCORPIO

- I am brave and passionate.

- I can be kind of secretive sometimes.

- If there's a problem, I can usually figure out how to solve it.

- I hate it when someone lies to me.

- I don't have much trouble making decisions.

If you got 16 or more, you're probably a true Scorpio.

SAGITTARIUS

- I have a ton of energy, and I always want to explore new things.

- I'm really interested in why people are the way they are, and why the world is the way it is.

- I can be kind of impatient.

- Sometimes I accidentally hurt people's feelings by saying what I think, when maybe I shouldn't.

- I need my freedom—I can't stand it when people try to keep me from doing what I want.

If you got 16 or more, you're probably a true Sagittarius.

CAPRICORN

- I'm very responsible—people can count on me.

- I know how to have a good time, but I can be pretty serious, too.

- I take a lot of pleasure in a job well done.

- I love Christmas and Halloween and
all the traditions that come with them.

- Sometimes I have a hard time seeing
someone else's perspective.

If you got 16 or more, you're probably a true Capricorn.

AQUARIUS

- I can be a little shy.

- I can usually see both sides of an argument
and find the way to what's right.

- I love hanging out with my friends,
but I really need my alone time, too.

- People might think I'm a little aloof,
until they get to know me.

- I really want to help other people.

If you got 16 or more, you're probably a true Aquarius.

PISCES

- I'm very artistic—and I love music.

- I am not at all judgmental, and I forgive really easily.

- I need a lot of sleep.

- I am very compassionate,
and I'm a good and faithful friend.

- I really value my alone time.

If you got 16 or more, you're probably a true Pisces.

Okay! Now that you know which sign is yours, you can use information about it as a guide for how to manage most life situations. Again, it's not a rulebook, and not all the advice will apply to you specifically, but you'll find that you recognize yourself most of the time. A little awareness of your style will help you navigate everything from school to friendships and family.

Managing School

No matter what your sign is, school can be a challenge—but it can also be great, even if it doesn't always feel like it. There's a lot of academic pressure, and a lot of time spent learning how to juggle a number of responsibilities—like when different teachers assign you several hours' worth of homework on the same night or when you've forgotten about a test coming up or when you just don't understand the assignment.

Everyone has strengths and weaknesses. Some of us are more organized than others, while some of us can think faster on our feet. It's just a matter of figuring out what you're good at and doing more of that, then figuring out what you're maybe not so good at and coming up with ways to be better. The cool thing is, these strengths and weaknesses are often directly related to your sign, and understanding them a little better can help you find a good strategy to get things done.

Harnessing Your Strengths

Aries

As a pretty competitive person, you are usually *great* in school, particularly in subjects that require a lot of debate or group projects. Use your natural leadership to motivate the others in your group and so you can make sure that the project gets done—and gets done well. You're great at coming up with solutions to complicated problems—trust your instincts!

Taurus

You work so hard, and it shows. Your teachers love you. You are great at coming up with a routine—so stick with it! And be sure to reward yourself regularly when you get something done. You're really good at staying organized.

Gemini

You're superdriven, and when you're interested in a topic, you blow everyone away. You're a great writer, and so you do really well in classes that require a lot of writing. And you're great at presentations, too. You have a lot of great ideas to contribute to group projects—don't be shy about them!

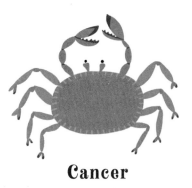

Cancer

You make sure your work gets *done,* even if sometimes you leave it to the last minute. You're always well-prepared, and you have a good imagination, too—when you've got a big project to do, it turns out really well and really cool.

Leo

When you're excited about something, you work really hard at it, and you can get everyone else excited about it, too! You're especially good at creative projects, and you put your own special touch on everything you do. You work well in a group, particularly if you're in charge.

Virgo

You're such a perfectionist, it's no wonder you do so well! You're methodical and detail-oriented, and you care more about doing things right than getting the grade—though that's certainly nice, too. Your analytical brain makes you great at math and science—anything logic-based is definitely your jam.

Libra

You love school for the sake of learning, and you work really well with group projects, particularly if everyone is doing their fair share. You're great at organizing, at managing disputes, and you're always there to help somebody else understand something they're not quite getting.

Scorpio

You are persistent and self-motivated. You hardly ever procrastinate. You always spot the trick question, and you're pretty good at guessing when there's a pop quiz coming. You often go deep, learning not just the assignment, but everything there is to know about the subject.

Sagittarius

You're curious about so many things, so most of the time school is pretty interesting. You know how to bring the fun to group projects, while still getting your work done. You take risks, and they usually pay off.

Capricorn

You take school really seriously—and so you should! You follow the assignments carefully and make sure they are done right. In group projects, you're the one who can get everyone to focus and pay attention.

Aquarius

You're terrific at creative projects, and you're really good at science and technology, too! You bring a lot of imagination and flair to your work, and it really stands out. You always want to try new ways of doing things, and you're often really engaged in class discussions.

Pisces

You love bringing your very best to your work, particularly when it's creative. You know that school is important, and so you work hard, even when it's not always that interesting. You have a lot of cool ideas, and people respond to them.

QUIZ

WHAT ARE YOUR STRENGTHS?

1. In group projects, I . . .

a) Make sure the job gets done.

b) Make sure everyone is having a good time while we work so hard.

c) Come up with a lot of good ideas.

d) Make sure everyone is doing their fair share.

2. When it's time to start homework, I . . .

a) Get going right away.

b) If it's something I'm really interested in, I'll start right away.
   Otherwise . . . I might procrastinate a little, but I'll get it done.

c) Definitely procrastinate. But I get it done!

d) If it's something I'm excited about, I'll do it right away. Or maybe
   I'll think about it for a while, and then start. If it's something I'm
   not interested in, maybe I'll get it over with, or I might procrastinate
   forever. It depends.

3. For me, school represents . . .

a) My future.

b) A chance to shine.

c) Something to do, and do well, so I can get on with my life.

d) A bit of a struggle, unless we're working on something I'm really into.

4. My best subjects are . . .

a) All of them. Hey, I work hard.

b) The ones I'm good at. I hate the other ones.

c) English, language arts, social studies, history . . . anything with a lot of writing.

d) I'm best at art, foreign language, and sometimes science and math, too.

Mostly A's (Earth Signs): You are dedicated and ambitious. Your strengths lie in your ability to focus and *get it done*.

Mostly B's (Fire Signs): You already know what your strengths are—and good thing, too, because you *love* what you're good at. When you're doing something that allows you to shine, it feels great, and then you do even better.

Mostly C's (Water Signs): You've got a great imagination—trust it! When you push yourself, you're amazing, and when you connect emotionally with what you're working on, you are a rock star.

Mostly D's (Air Signs): You're great at a lot of different things, particularly when you can stay focused. When you get to be creative, you have a lot of fun—and that's when you do your best work.

Strengthening
Your Weaknesses

ARIES

You can get a little frustrated sometimes, even with your teacher—particularly if you feel like maybe you could be doing something else, something that's a little more fun. Instead of butting heads, see if you can rein in your temper and make something that feels boring into something more interesting. Your need to move quickly can sometimes lead to tiny mistakes—slow down a little bit!

TAURUS

Make sure to cut yourself some slack sometimes! You don't have to do everything perfectly to be a great student—mistakes can happen to anybody, even you. Sometimes the best way to avoid errors is to take a break. Remember, you are more methodical than others, and so will move at your own pace. This is a *good* thing.

GEMINI

You tend to have trouble focusing, and sometimes it can seem like there is no good answer. If you're hanging out with friends doing homework together, you're never going to get anything done because it's so much more fun to laugh. Then again, if you shut yourself up in your room so you can focus, you just hate it. Find a good middle ground, maybe studying with just a friend or two or at the kitchen table at home.

CANCER

You need your alone time. You learn best when you can focus and really think about something. But you do have a tendency to procrastinate, so make sure you allow yourself the time you need—don't leave everything until the last minute!

LEO

You tend to rush through projects, not because you're not interested, but since you're so excited. Don't get so carried away with an idea that you miss the details. Double-check your work.

VIRGO

Play into your strengths! Keep your desk nice and neat, and get some fun colored pens to take notes with. If something interrupts your routine, try not to let it throw you—and don't be so hard on yourself!

LIBRA

You have a tendency to leave things until the last minute. See if you can take a tip from Virgo and set yourself a schedule. Snack, then homework, then free time? Reward yourself when you get something done—but you do have to get it done first.

SCORPIO

You could be at the top of your class, if you want to. When something interests you, you really go for it . . . but if it doesn't, you tend to zone out. Is it possible that something you think is boring could be interesting after all? Maybe just check it out and see . . .

SAGITTARIUS

Settle down, there! Yes, there are so many fascinating and fun things in the world, but sometimes you won't get to them unless you get through the not-so-fun stuff first. Don't push your work off until the last minute—get it done, so you can go on to better things.

CAPRICORN

Creative projects aren't always your jam. It can be hard to know what's expected of you and difficult to be sure you're doing it "right." But there isn't always a right way and a wrong way! See if you can go with the flow a little and explore your artsy side—you might enjoy it more than you think!

AQUARIUS

It can look really chaotic from the outside, but you actually do know what you're doing. Your unusual, haphazard study techniques work for you. If someone is pushing you to be more structured, prove to them that you can do it your way—but then you have to really nail it.

PISCES

Participating in class is maybe not your favorite thing. You're a little shy, and everybody else is noisy and yelling—and what if you say the wrong thing? Try not to worry so much. *Everybody* says the wrong thing sometimes, and you've seen how it doesn't do them any harm. See if you can push past your shyness, just a little.

MEDITATION FOR FOCUS

This meditation will help you get yourself in the right frame of mind for studying. If you feel yourself getting distracted or if you're just having a hard time focusing, take a break and try this meditation—and then get back to work! Recommended for Aries, Gemini, Cancer, Leo, Libra, Scorpio, Sagittarius, and Aquarius.

Start by getting away from distractions. This might mean finding a little space away from your friends, putting away any devices, turning off the music—just get yourself a little quiet time.

If your eyes want to close, let them, but don't force it. If you're having to screw your eyes shut to keep them closed, try just lowering your eyelids or letting your gaze blur a little.

Take ten deep breaths, concentrating on each one. Breathe in slowly through your nose, and feel the air puff up your chest and move down into your belly. Exhale out through the mouth, and pay attention to your warm breath as it leaves your body.

If your mind starts to wander, that's okay—just guide yourself back to your breath.

If your eyes are ready to close now, let them. Take ten more deep breaths, this time sitting up straighter as you inhale and feeling your body rooted to the earth as you exhale. Feel the clarity that each breath brings—new oxygen, new life, new energy—and release all the distractions with each exhale.

MEDITATION TO STRENGTHEN
YOUR CREATIVITY

This meditation will help you tap into your imagination and your intuition, to help you when you feel a bit overwhelmed and like you don't know where to start. Recommended for Taurus, Virgo, Capricorn, and Pisces.

This meditation practice may feel a little unusual, since it's not asking you to sit and think about nothing. Instead, it's a little more like intentional daydreaming. It's fun!

You'll want to be in a relatively peaceful place for this, but it doesn't need to be silent. You just want to go where nobody's going to try and talk to you for a little while.

For a moment, don't do anything at all. Just sit and look around. What do you see? Are people going about their business all around you? Are you outside? Even if you're just looking at a blank wall, what do you notice? Look at the texture of the paint.

After a little while, if your eyes want to close, let them—but if not, that's okay. Now listen. What do you hear? Are there birds chirping, someone coughing, someone laughing? Can you hear the sound of a fan or a breeze?

What do you feel? Can you feel the air blowing against your face? Is it cool? Is your seat comfortable? Become aware of everything that's going on around you.

And then, start to let it all go. Stop paying so much attention to everything *outside* of you, and see what's going on *inside*. What springs to mind? It can be anything at all—just let yourself think of something you like, something that excites you. Daydream about it a little, and feel that excitement start to permeate your body.

Finally, let that excitement—the energy you've created in your head—come out with you into the world. You've sparked your imagination—now bring its light out from within and see what it shows you.

Events to Be Aware Of

MERCURY RETROGRADE

As the planet responsible for communication, Mercury is normally extremely helpful when it comes to school! But three or four times a year, for around three weeks each time, Mercury starts moving in the opposite direction from us in our journey around the sun.

Now, that might seem like nonsense. Don't all the planets in the solar system travel in the same direction? Absolutely. But they don't all do it at the same speed. Think about when you're driving down the highway—you know how when you pass a really slow car, it looks almost like that car is going backward? That is what's happening with our planet and Mercury, and it pretty much makes everything go haywire.

Technology gets a little screwed up, so something you've emailed may not arrive. An assignment you're *sure* you did turns out somehow to have not gotten done, and you tend to misplace things.

This is just the deal when Mercury is in retrograde, and there's not much you can do except wait it out. During this time, double-check everything, and really take your time!

It should be noted that every planet goes retrograde, and that can have an impact—but none are felt so profoundly as Mercury, which is why it gets called out all the time.

SOLAR ECLIPSE

A solar eclipse is when the moon stands between us and the sun for a period of time. Most often, it just covers part of the sun—a partial solar eclipse—but every eighteen months, there is a full solar eclipse somewhere in the world. If it's where you are, it's definitely worth experiencing. The light outside gets very odd. And if you can view it safely with special blackout lenses, it looks like the moon is on fire. Using a pinhole projector where you watch the light and moving shadow on a clear surface is also very cool. It's no wonder such a spectacular and dramatic event can cause some upheaval. Whether a solar eclipse is full or partial, it does tend to stir things up! A solar eclipse generally marks the end of something—and the beginning of something else. In the case of school, that could mean wrapping up a project, or it could be something bigger—like you realizing a new talent or aptitude.

LUNAR ECLIPSE

A lunar eclipse occurs when the earth comes between the sun and the moon. This happens much more often than a solar eclipse—there are between two and five lunar eclipses every year. During a lunar eclipse, the moon becomes shadowed, almost disappearing before your eyes. Like a solar eclipse, a lunar eclipse marks beginnings and endings—but because the moon rules over our emotions, these beginnings and endings tend to cause a lot of *feelings*. If you find yourself getting emotional at school, make sure to give yourself a break. You can ask your teacher or counselor for a little space—and know that it's going to be okay. This too shall pass.

Managing Friends

Navigating friendship is like trying to make your way through a stormy sea without a compass—you just never know what is going to happen next. But being aware of the dynamics of astrology can help you figure out how you tend to react to certain situations and how your friends do, too. Your friendships can be the most rewarding and fun relationships of your life, but they can also be the most challenging. For example, using the knowledge you have about how Pisceans respond to arguments or how an Aquarian isn't really being flaky can keep those friendships sailing on smooth seas.

How to Be a Great Friend

ARIES

When you like someone, you make sure they know it! You are generous with compliments and affection, and you love to go out and do things with your friends. Make sure you remain patient with those who aren't quite as energetic as you are, and pay attention to whether you're being overly bossy. You know it happens sometimes!

TAURUS

Your friends can always rely on you. You are a calming influence. Because you always know what's really going on, you can help your friends see through their own confusion. But make sure, little bull, that you don't give in to your natural stubbornness—other people have good ideas, too!

GEMINI

You love having a big circle of friends, and because you are able to see so many different points of view, you tend to like a wide variety of people. Just make sure you give yourself the space and freedom to spend some time alone. If you don't, you're likely to get overwhelmed by all the demands on your time.

CANCER

Your naturally empathetic nature makes you such a good listener, it's no wonder so many of your friends love you so! Remember that they might not all be as emotionally mature as you are—or as willing to talk about their feelings and their experience. Try not to let your feelings get hurt by this; different people handle their emotions differently.

LEO

You are so much fun! You are goofy and charismatic, and whether you notice it or not, people are always paying attention to what you're doing. Make sure you are paying attention back, because sometimes you can hurt feelings without meaning to.

VIRGO

Your caring nature means that you are always the person your friends call when there's a problem—and you're always capable of handling that problem! Whether it's for advice or just a listening ear, your friends can depend on you. But if you don't pay attention, you'll end up feeling resentful, because you'll start feeling like you do all the work. Remember, you get to ask for help, too.

LIBRA

Your thoughtfulness and ability to understand all sides of a situation make you a valuable friend, and don't ever doubt it! Sometimes, your shyness might keep you from feeling like you can let your friends really know who you are. Trust them!

SCORPIO

It takes a little bit of work to get past your protective shell, but once someone works their way into your affections, you are an amazing friend. You are fiercely loyal and will stand up for your friends in any situation. Try to take a little advice from Libra and remember that there are two sides to every story—and you might not always be right.

SAGITTARIUS

Your sense of adventure and fun draws people to you—particularly people who want to follow along with your interests. You're optimistic, and if someone doesn't get you, that's fine, because you're on to the next thing! Make sure you stop and look occasionally, though, because you might be missing out on something (or someone) great.

CAPRICORN

You are reliable and loyal, and your friends love you for it. You're the planner of the group, which is good because otherwise you all might just sit around all day! Allow yourself to have fun, too—you can't be responsible for everyone!

AQUARIUS

You're imaginative and fun, and you have a big heart—you really care about the world around you. You can get a little stuck in your head sometimes, and your friends might think you're mad at them for something. Make sure to let them know that you aren't! This is just how you are.

PISCES

You are a dreamer and a lover. You idealize your friends, but you also know exactly who they are—you can help them become the very best version of themselves. You are so easygoing, though, that sometimes your friends might take advantage of you without even realizing it.

WHAT KIND OF A FRIEND
ARE YOU?

1. When I'm hanging out with a group of people, I . . .

a) Like to pick one or two people to stick with.

b) Tend to be the center of attention, whether I mean to or not.

c) Pay attention to what's going on with everyone—I can always tell what the social dynamics are.

d) Move around a lot, talk to this person, then that person. I like to circulate!

2. When a friend has a problem, I . . .

a) Start by helping them calm down. It's hardly ever as bad as they think it is.

b) Immediately rush to their side. We will work it out together.

c) Feel it like it's happening to me, too.

d) Might wait to see if it blows over before I get all worked up about it.

3. For me, friendship represents . . .

a) Community. We have each other's backs.

b) People who make me happy!

c) The people I truly care about.

d) New ideas, new ways of thinking, new energy.

4. I am the best at . . .

a) Support. My friends can always count on me.

b) Bringing the fun! I always make sure everyone has a good time.

c) Listening. My friends know they can tell me anything.

d) Kindness. I am always able to put myself in someone else's shoes.

Mostly A's (Earth Signs): You are a calming, caring influence for your friends. You are always there for them, and you almost always have a solution to every problem. When you choose someone as a friend, you are giving them a huge gift.

Mostly B's (Fire Signs): You just want to make sure everyone is happy, including you! But that doesn't mean you're not around for the hard stuff—when the going gets tough, you are always right there, fighting alongside your friends.

Mostly C's (Water Signs): Your compassion and loving heart makes you the most thoughtful friend anyone could have. You celebrate your friends' successes as if they were your own, and you would do anything for them.

Mostly D's (Air Signs): While you can be a little hard to make plans with, you are always a delight to be around. You make everything so much more interesting.

What to Do When a Friendship Isn't Working

Certain signs just have a hard time bonding with one another. It doesn't mean they can never be friends, or that these aren't extremely valuable relationships—it just means that maybe they require a little more intention and work than others.

ARIES

You can have a tough time with Capricorn, Cancer, and sometimes Pisces or other Aries. When that happens, try to check your own impulses—are you being too fiery? Are you being impatient? And then, play to your strengths! You are incredibly honest about both the positives and the negatives of any situation. Show your affection, and then have a heart-to-heart about the friendship.

TAURUS

You tend to butt heads with Leo, Aquarius, some Aries, and often other Tauruses. When these signs are asking you to be more flexible than you like, how can you work with that? If you feel like your needs are never being respected, then you can talk about that—but you should also consider that maybe you can go with the flow a bit more.

GEMINI

You can get along with pretty much anybody, but if you do get irritated, it tends to be by a Virgo, a Pisces, or sometimes a Taurus or another Gemini. If that's the case, it's often because you, dear Gemini, are taking on qualities of someone else that don't feel right for you—or you're being annoyed by behavior that is too like your own. Have a look inside. Probably what you need is a break, and you should take it before things get out of hand.

CANCER

Aries, Libra, and sometimes Gemini or another Cancer can hurt your feelings from time to time. Your sensitive nature makes this likely—but you shouldn't necessarily blame yourself. When someone is being thoughtless, you need to let them know. They probably didn't mean it, but their behavior won't change unless you talk to them about it.

LEO

Scorpio and Taurus, as well as Cancer or another Leo, don't always recognize how vulnerable you are, deep down. Remember, you hide it well, so you can't necessarily expect them to get it! Rather than becoming angry and lashing out, take a deep breath. You've done the same thing to others—is it possible you've done it this time, as well? The good news is, you're very good at apologizing and at asking for what you need.

VIRGO

You can feel taken advantage of by Gemini, Sagittarius, and sometimes Leo or another Virgo. You do so much for other people, and these signs occasionally have a tendency to simply not realize it and give you the credit you're due. Odds are they aren't doing it on purpose, though. Don't let your resentment simmer. You can change your behavior and do a little less for them.

LIBRA

Cancer, Capricorn, and sometimes Virgo or another Libra can occasionally push at your boundaries. You have strong opinions on what is right and wrong—and what is fair and unfair—but you don't always communicate them clearly. If someone is doing something you feel is wrong, speak up.

SCORPIO

Your sense of innate reserve can confuse Leo, Aquarius, and sometimes Libra or another Scorpio, and they may react badly. The truth is, they probably feel like you don't like them. Make an effort to open up a little bit more. It really is worth it.

SAGITTARIUS

Virgo, Pisces, and sometimes Scorpio or another Sagittarius may be thrown by your carefree outlook. You know it doesn't mean you don't feel things deeply or understand what matters, but they might find it hard to see that. Take a bit of time to reassure those around you.

CAPRICORN

You sometimes have a hard time getting along with Aries, Libra, and sometimes Sagittarius or another Capricorn. You are very focused, and sometimes that can come off as distant or unwilling to compromise. The truth is that you feel things very deeply, but don't always want to have a discussion. Push at that boundary a little bit, and see if maybe you can let other people in just a bit closer.

AQUARIUS

Your creative and somewhat loosey-goosey nature can be a little confusing to Taurus, Scorpio, or even Capricorn or another Aquarius. They are often more structured than you are, and you can feel like you just don't get each other. But you love having a wide variety of friends and interests—take a minute to see what they have to offer!

PISCES

You don't always mix well with Gemini, Sagittarius, Aquarius, or even another Pisces. You are so sweet and loving, but your chill, "it will happen when it happens" attitude can feel frustrating or even dismissive to your friends who are a little more action-oriented. When you make plans together, make sure you stick to them!

MEDITATION FOR COMPASSION

This meditation will help you see other people's point of view and work to meet them where they are. Recommended for Aries, Taurus, Leo, Scorpio, Sagittarius, and Capricorn.

The first step of compassion is awareness. We cannot feel empathy for what someone else is experiencing unless we notice it—and we cannot become aware of someone else's experience without first asking ourselves what *we* are feeling.

So start with a little mindfulness meditation for yourself. Close or soften the eyes, and sit with your body. What are you feeling physically? Feel yourself breathing, and feel any aches or vibrations or itches you might be experiencing. And then go deeper—what are you sensing emotionally? What's going on for you?

Once you've flexed that awareness muscle a little, extend it out to your friend. Now, we can't actually know for sure what other people are feeling or experiencing, but we can imagine based on how we would feel in a similar circumstance. Think about what is going on in your friend's life. Think about how that would make you feel, both physically and emotionally.

Now think about the ways in which you are different from your friend. How might this affect how they are feeling?

Take a minute to imagine a cord connecting the two of you. That cord represents the things you have in common, the things you like about each other—all the reasons you are friends with one another. Pour some energy into it.

When you're ready, open your eyes, and maybe take a moment to send your friend a quick text or hello, just to let them know you're thinking about them.

MEDITATION FOR BOUNDARIES

This meditation will help you think about what you need and get con-fident asking for what you want. Recommended for Gemini, Cancer, Virgo, Libra, Aquarius, and Pisces.

Close or soften your eyes, and sit comfortably. Pay attention to your breath as you breathe in and out. Once you've got a good rhythm going, feel your body pressing into the earth. Pay atten-tion to all the places you are literally being supported by the world around you.

From the bottom up, imagine a column of white light sur-rounding you. This gentle barrier will let in only what you want it to, and it will release only what you let it. In this safe place, think about what you really need from your friend. What do you feel you aren't getting?

What would it feel like to talk to them about that? How scary would it be, really? Imagine having that conversation. Imagine it going as badly as it possibly could—remember, you're protected by that column of white light.

Is that really how it would go? Now, imagine it going as well as it possibly could.

The reality is that it will probably be somewhere in the middle. Can you live with that?

When you're ready, carefully lower your column of white light, knowing that you can call it up at any time. Open your eyes.

Events to Be Aware Of

MERCURY RETROGRADE

Communication is the most important thing in a friendship—and when Mercury goes into retrograde, that can make things go haywire! But this can be a time of opportunity. When communication is at its worst, what can you see? Is it *just* Mercury retrograde, or is this an ongoing problem? If you feel like you're just not being heard—or if everything you say is being misinterpreted—then maybe the problem isn't with the stars. Pay attention, and see if you can find out.

SOLAR ECLIPSE

Solar eclipses can be times of upheaval for friendships—but that isn't necessarily a bad thing. If a friendship has turned toxic, a solar eclipse will let you know. But a solar eclipse is also a time of new beginnings, signifying either the start of a new friendship or a new commitment to an older friendship.

LUNAR ECLIPSE

If you find yourself having a lot of heavy emotional conversations with your friends, there's probably a lunar eclipse going on. It's okay. Even if that sort of thing is really uncomfortable for you, remember—your friends are the people it's safe to be emotional with, and they're going through the same kinds of things you are. Be there for each other.

Managing Family

Our families are the most important things in our lives. They can be the source of our greatest joys and our greatest form of support—and they can drive us absolutely crazy. The reality of living day to day with other people is that there are always ups and downs no matter how much we love each other.

One of the most frequent challenges we face is trying to convince our parents that we know what we are doing. It can be hard for them to adjust when they remember they had to show us how to walk. But now we are older, and we want to try and stretch our wings!

How to Convince Your Parents You've Got This

ARIES

Fierce Aries, *of course* you can handle anything that's thrown at you. But not everybody is going to get that from the beginning. Maybe the best way to convince your parents is to show them that you can be chill—just do your thing without pushing and allow your parents to see just how capable you are.

TAURUS

Sometimes, you have to try things someone else's way in order for them to trust that you can do it *your* way. For example, if you show that you can listen to their advice, your parents will be more willing to hear what you have to say. It's hard—and may feel incredibly frustrating—but it'll probably save time if you go along rather than digging in your heels.

GEMINI

Making decisions isn't always your strong suit, but it's an important part of handling whatever comes up. Practice making choices on your own for a little while so that your folks can see that your inner compass is reliable—and then you'll learn to trust it, too.

CANCER

You care so much about other people that your parents are going to worry about you—they'll wonder if you know how to put yourself first when you really need to. Show them you can maintain good boundaries.

LEO

Leo, all you need to do is not get carried away! You come up with some crazy ideas sometimes, and while they usually work out, maybe they don't *seem* like they will. Rein it in for a little while, and then slowly expand so your parents can get used to your wild ways.

VIRGO

Your parents probably trust you more than you think—maybe even more than you trust yourself! If you feel like they don't, consider talking about it with them. Whatever their concerns are, your practical nature should be able to set their minds at rest.

LIBRA

Spending time with your friends is so important to you, and your parents know this . . . but they probably also miss you sometimes! If you feel like they're not letting you go out as often as you like, consider how often that really is. It might be that you're going out way more than you think.

SCORPIO

You're a very private person, and you like to do things on your own. So it probably drives you crazy when your parents get into your business. Try to remember that as far as they're concerned, minding your business is their literal *job*. They're just trying to handle this whole parenting thing, and it isn't easy. Let them in a little bit, and they'll loosen their grip on you.

SAGITTARIUS

You long for the freedom to do anything you want to, whenever you want—but you're not an adult yet. Unfortunately, you don't quite have the freedom you want. But if you slow down and talk to your parents about the things you want to do, perhaps they'll start to say yes more often.

CAPRICORN

You're so responsible, so it probably feels ridiculous that anyone wouldn't trust you completely. Your parents should know you can handle your own life! And the truth is they probably do, but they may also feel like they need to keep a close eye just in case . . . It's not because of anything to do with you, but that's what parents need to do sometimes. Let them know how that makes you feel, and see if they back off a little.

AQUARIUS

You can be a little lost in the clouds sometimes, so maybe it isn't *so* unreasonable for your parents to want to keep an eye out for you. If you work to stay grounded and pay attention to the small stuff, they'll start to notice and won't feel like they need to hover so much.

PISCES

You don't really go out all that often, so when you do, it makes sense that you want to have some freedom! If your parents are really standing in your way, talk to them about that. It might be a little uncomfortable for you, but it's worth it.

QUIZ

HAVE YOU GOT THIS?

1. When I'm getting ready to go somewhere, I . . .

a) Always make sure my phone is charged, and I already know how I'm going to get there.

b) Look *fantastic*. Even if it means I'm running a little late.

c) Wait around for everyone else . . . Even if we're slow getting going, we should all go together!

d) Get there eventually? And maybe get lost on the way . . .

2. When my parents ask me where I'm going, I . . .

a) Give them the location, the names of the people I will be with, and a firm ETA of when I'll be back.

b) Tell them only what they really need to know.

c) Don't always know how to answer them. We might be doing one thing, but we might decide to do something else . . .

d) Am a little vague, but only because I want to keep my options open!

3. If I run into trouble, I . . .

a) Have a backup plan. And a backup plan to my backup plan.

b) Come up with a solution. I'm great at thinking on my feet.

c) Know I can always call on someone for help.

d) Don't always know what to do, to be honest.

4. If I get put in a situation that makes me uncomfortable, I . . .

a) Just keep my head down until it's over.

b) Get out of it. Who has time for that?

c) Try to take care of it.

d) Just disappear. I might stay but not talk to anybody, or I might get home on my own: I'm not going to be confrontational.

Mostly A's (Earth Signs): You have *definitely* got this. You're pre-pared. You know what you're doing. And you help everyone else fig-ure things out, too. One thing you could maybe work on is allowing a little more flexibility—sometimes things don't go quite the way you plan, but maybe it'll be even better?

Mostly B's (Fire Signs): Slow down and take a breath. You are great at making quick decisions, but not everyone can keep up with you. There might be some better options available if you take a moment to think about them.

Mostly C's (Water Signs): There are going to be times when your friends are wrong or when they won't know how to handle things. Can you step up when that happens? Someone will have to . . .

Mostly D's (Air Signs): While being flexible is definitely a good thing, it's not a bad idea to have a plan. It can be annoying to have to think about practical things, but if you force yourself to come up with a structure, you'll find that you actually have *more* freedom to do what you want.

How to Let the People You Love Know It

With so much going on in our lives, it can be hard to be truly available—particularly with family. But they love us and we love them, so it's important to make sure everybody knows it.

ARIES

You're intense and passionate, and you like to *do* things—so do them with family! It's probably been a while since the people you live with really felt your light shining on them. Take some time to plan a family activity or adventure! It'll be a great bonding experience.

TAURUS

When you love someone, all you want is to spend time with them. So just hang out with your family. It doesn't have to be anything special or fancy. You're happiest when you all play a board game or even just watch a movie together.

GEMINI

You're an incredibly good listener. So when was the last time you checked in on everybody? Ask what's going on in your parents' or your siblings' lives. You'll probably find you have a lot more in common these days than you think.

CANCER

You love taking care of people, and you probably do it all the time. But when was the last time you let someone take care of you? That's a way to show love, too, you know . . .

LEO

You are a problem-solver extraordinaire, and no situation is too big or too small for you to jump right into. So get on it! There's always some advice you can give . . . and if that fails, throw a family dance party. They'll complain, but they'll secretly love it.

VIRGO

You love to be helpful, but have you thought about just taking it easy? Sometimes all anyone wants from you is to *be* with you, enjoying each other's company. You don't always have to be doing things.

LIBRA

It's so easy for families to fall into habits of not communicating, often without meaning to or even realizing they are doing it. Tell everyone to get off their phones! You love to chat and have great conversations, so make it happen.

SCORPIO

Alone time is important to you, but have you considered lately how it makes the people around you feel? They might think you're mad at them or upset about something, especially if they don't value solitude the way you do. You don't have to spend *all* your time with your family, but come out of your hermit cave sometimes, just to let everyone know you're still around.

SAGITTARIUS

You are so much fun! Let your fam in on the good times . . . You don't need to go anywhere or do anything—though that's certainly not a bad idea. You can make an ordinary evening or afternoon fun just by letting your high spirits soar.

CAPRICORN

Stay in touch with your family throughout the day. It doesn't need to be anything big—just texting a joke or a meme or even just saying hi. These small gestures can make an enormous difference.

AQUARIUS

Think about it—when was the last time you said, "I love you"? You probably think you show it all the time, but sometimes people need to hear you say it.

PISCES

True connection is so important to you—as it should be! But sometimes you forget that the simple, everyday interactions can be meaningful, too. Watching a show together, going on a dive through YouTube, or even just being near each other can help maintain closeness.

MEDITATION TO CARVE OUT
SPACE FOR YOURSELF

This meditation will help you create the mental and energetic space you need to be there for others. Recommended for Leo, Virgo, Scorpio, Sagittarius, Aquarius, and Pisces, but honestly any sign would benefit from this.

The first step to creating mental and energetic space is to start with physical space. This can be particularly hard if you share a room with someone else. But even if you have your own room, is it really conducive to meditation? If you're sharing a room, make sure that part of that shared space is yours alone. Clear out anything that intrudes on that boundary—so clothes, books, or just general *stuff* that isn't yours should be gently shifted aside.

Once your space is your own, take a minute to clear it out. Tidy things up, make your bed—do what you can to organize things so that you can feel calm and peaceful. Then light a candle or some incense or diffuse some essential oils—whatever makes you feel like you can breathe a little more easily, with a little more peace.

And then, just take some time for yourself. Let everyone know that you need a little alone time, and spend it doing whatever is most helpful for *you*. That can mean meditating, but it can also mean journaling, drawing, writing, or simply daydreaming. This isn't a time to scroll through your phone or text your friends—this is a pause that is meant to fill you up, not drain you. Give yourself the space you need to just *be yourself*—for yourself and no one else.

MEDITATION TO KEEP CALM
AND LOOK FOR THE GOOD

Everybody gets stressed out sometimes . . . And unfortunately, with so many different kinds of people living under one roof, home can sometimes be the most stressful place of all. This meditation will help you find your inner calm so that you can find the good in others, even when they are at their worst. Recommended for Aries, Taurus, Gemini, Cancer, Libra, and Capricorn, but any sign would benefit.

Start by taking a deep breath. No matter where you are and no matter what's happening around you, just breathe. Right at this moment, maybe that's all you can manage, and that's okay. But as soon as you can, take a step away from the situation that is keeping you from being calm. Go find a quiet corner.

Sit down on the floor if you can, and really try and feel it beneath you. Feel the way your ankles press into the rug or tile or wood or whatever it is you're sitting on. Notice the sensation. Where are your hands? Are they in your lap, resting on your knees, or down at your sides? There's no right answer here, just take note of what is going on in your body.

And now, see if you can intentionally slow down your heartbeat. Keep taking those deep breaths, and keep feeling into your body. Once your heart rate has slowed and your breath is coming more easily, try to turn your thoughts away from the situation. This might be hard, but give it a try. Try to think of other moments in your home, moments of peace and easy happiness. They happen all the time, we just don't notice them as much as the difficult ones.

Know that thinking about the good things doesn't mean that whatever situation that has cropped up isn't hard or that it doesn't need to be addressed. But making the effort to think about an easier time can allow you the emotional space to have a thoughtful conversation, rather than a reactive or angry one.

Events to Be Aware Of

MERCURY RETROGRADE

Ugh, Mercury, could you please just keep it together? Communication with families is hard enough without you screwing everything up with your wacky orbit.

But Mercury's going to do Mercury, and there's nothing we can do about it. Make sure to be overly communicative during this time—double-check to make sure you haven't missed any texts or emails from your parents, call when you're running late, and be patient when *they* don't communicate well with you.

SOLAR ECLIPSE

No matter what kind of changes come your way, your family will always, *always* be there. That can feel like a bad thing sometimes, especially if you're going through a period when you just don't seem to get each other, but maybe a solar eclipse will help change that! Solar eclipses are great for helping everyone realize and understand something they'd never really considered before. So maybe this would be a good time to take advantage of that and talk to your family about something you've been putting off discussing?

LUNAR ECLIPSE

Everybody gets emotional during a lunar eclipse, and that can mean a whole lot of feelings under one roof. Try not to take it all too seriously—people can believe the things they say they're feeling during a lunar eclipse, but once that time has passed, they may find they don't really feel that way after all. Has this ever happened to you? Maybe you've thought, "My brother is so selfish; I don't even think he's a good person." But then he does something nice, and you remember why you really do love him.

Consider that this kind of thing can happen with others in your family, too, and give them a pass if they say something it turns out they don't mean.

PART II

The Signs

We've looked at how knowing your sign can help you figure out how to deal with particular situations, but now let's backtrack and get a better global view of each sign. Exploring your sign—and those of your family and friends—from a few different angles will give you a clearer picture of the things that influence your personality.

What's the big picture for each sign? What other signs and elements do they really mesh with? What are the decans for each sign and how do these affect their personality types? All these questions will be answered. We'll take a look at the life of one inspirational person per sign to get a sense of how they embody the characteristics of that sign. And then, for added fun, we can try out a variety of crafts that speak to a certain aspect of each sign.

Ready to uncover more about yourself? Let's go!

Aries

MARCH 21–APRIL 19

• • • • •

As the first of the Fire Signs—and also the first of all the signs—Aries is a leader in all things. You are *extremely* energetic and confident, always looking for new adventures. You are a trailblazer and a trendsetter, and you push everyone around you to explore and achieve bigger and better things. You love life and want to experience everything—and be the best at everything. You never back down from a fight and will stand beside your friends to the end.

Your favorite color tends to be red. You love new clothes and roller coasters. You win most arguments. And you love applause.

You don't love to share. You hate being ignored. You're not a very good loser. And you often refuse to hear the word *no*.

Compatibility

- **FRIENDS WITH:** You're compatible with a number of signs: Gemini, Leo, Libra, and other Aries.
- **BEST FRIEND:** Your better half, the person who will complement

you, is likely to be an Air Sign, someone who will feed your fire, but won't compete with you for it. A Gemini in particular will share many interests with you, be happy to be led by you, and be able to keep up with your high energy.

Famous Aries

LEONARDO DA VINCI
April 15, 1452–May 2, 1519

"Iron rusts from disuse; water loses its purity from stagnation . . . even so does inaction sap the vigor of the mind."

Leonardo da Vinci is pretty much the original genius. He either studied or pioneered work in math, geology, astronomy, engineering, botany, paleontology, and cartography. If he thought of something useful but it didn't exist, he invented it. The helicopter, tank, parachute, and calculator are all based on his inventions, and he also dabbled in solar power.

Plus, you know, he was an incredible artist. Sure, the *Mona Lisa* is his most famous painting, but his other paintings—not to mention his drawings and sculptures—were and are equally, if not more, beautiful.

You've probably heard about right brains and left brains—how the right brain dominates the creative side and the left brain dominates the science-y, logical side. It's rare for someone to be equally gifted in both, but da Vinci certainly was. During his time, he was valued more for his artistic works than his scientific ones. Because he hadn't been formally trained, contemporary mathematicians and scientists tended to be a bit dismissive of his contributions, at least for the first part of his life.

But da Vinci's worth was unmistakable, so much so that Francis I, the king of France, gave him a castle of his own—the Château d'Amboise—where he could work to his heart's content on whatever interested him the most. The story goes that he died in the arms of the king himself.

ARIES CRAFT:

Candle

You are the flaming leader of the zodiac, and so it is only appropriate for you to light the way. Making a candle is both fun and easy!

MATERIALS

+ ½ lb. soy or beeswax candle wax
+ Double boiler
+ Candlewicks
+ 8 oz. clean, clear jar
+ Bright, citrusy fragrance oil, or scent of your choice (optional)
+ Red candle dye
+ Wick holder
+ Acrylic paint pens

Slowly melt your wax in your double boiler. As it melts, dip the base of your wick into the liquid and quickly place the wick in the center of your jar and let it harden—this will help hold it in place when you're pouring your candle.

Once the wax has melted completely, remove it from the heat and stir in half an ounce of your fragrance oil and a little of your dye. (Check the package instructions for the dye as directions are often different, but a little often goes a long way.)

Run the outside of your jar under hot water to let it warm up a bit (this will help the wax adhere to the jar). Dry it off, and then carefully pour the wax into the jar, keeping the wick centered. Use the wick holder to keep the wick upright, and let the candle harden for one hour.

Once the glass has cooled entirely, take your paint pens and carefully draw the Aries constellation, zodiac symbol, or any other design of your choice on the jar to decorate your candle. Light your candle when you want to ignite your inner flame.

Events to Watch Out For

- **MOON IN ARIES.** The moon makes Aries even more impulsive than usual—so take care to think things through.
- **MERCURY IN ARIES.** Pause a moment before you talk when Mercury is hanging out in Aries.
- **MERCURY RETROGRADE.** When Mercury's orbit starts going a little wonky while it's in Aries, it might make you go a little

wonky, too. Your temper will be short, your patience will be limited, and your usually direct and confident nature will be confused. When these feelings do happen, just keep calm and take a lot of deep breaths. They will pass.

- **MARS IN ARIES.** When Mars is in Aries, you might feel a little too . . . intense. Your enthusiasms will become passions, and your passions will become obsessions. Be a little more chill, if you can.

Events to Look Forward To

- **SUN IN ARIES.** When the sun comes to Aries, the astrological year begins. That new beginning infuses Aries with even more enthusiasm and drive. This is why you always want to do something fun and new for your birthday!
- **VENUS IN ARIES.** Venus gives Aries a boost of self-confidence— so if there's someone you really want to get to know better, now's the time to reach out to them!

- **JUPITER IN ARIES.** Anything is possible! This is a time to reach for your dreams. They won't *always* work out, but the chances are pretty good now.
- **SATURN IN ARIES.** Saturn brings a sense of organization and responsibility to your usual impulsivity—this is a time when things will get done.
- **NEPTUNE IN ARIES.** Luckily for you, Neptune will visit your sign in the relatively near future. It takes fourteen years for Neptune to move from one sign to another, so this will be a big time for you. You'll be able to bring change to the world and make it a better place.

Decans

MARS DECAN
March 21–March 29

If you're born in the first third of the Aries sign, you're ruled by Mars, and so you are *especially* competitive. You also tend to get in a lot of fights. It's kind of like you're a regular Aries on steroids. But that means that your assertiveness will ensure that you will achieve every single one of your dreams and that you will have a profound impact on the world.

- **ASPECTS TO CELEBRATE.** You are fierce, energetic, and passionate. You inspire everyone around you.
- **ASPECTS TO USE WITH CAUTION.** You can be impatient and impulsive: you leap into situations without thinking them through. Also, keep an eye on that temper of yours, and make sure your battles are worth fighting.
- **POTENTIAL CAREERS.** Whatever you want!

SUN DECAN
March 30–April 8

If you're born in the second decan, you're ruled by the sun—and you are born to lead. You have the drive and enthusiasm of a typical Aries, along with strong charisma and a good sense of humor. You really like being the center of attention, which is nice, because you usually are! You have a kind heart and will use your powers for good.

- **ASPECTS TO CELEBRATE.** You have lots of friends who really adore you—and with good reason!
- **ASPECTS TO USE WITH CAUTION.** You can get a little braggy sometimes. Let that sense of humor shine through, and laugh at yourself.
- **POTENTIAL CAREERS.** You would be a great politician or head of a company.

JUPITER DECAN
April 9–April 19

If you're born in the third decan, you're ruled by Jupiter, which brings out your creativity and your generosity. You're social, fun-loving, and adventurous. You're always learning and exploring new things, meeting new people, and getting to know them. You're always the optimist, able to see the best in everything and everyone.

- **ASPECTS TO CELEBRATE.** You work hard but know how to let it all go and have a good time. You take so much joy in life.

- **ASPECTS TO USE WITH CAUTION.** You can be a little lost in your own world, and sometimes your optimism makes you have unrealistic expectations.

- **POTENTIAL CAREERS.** You would be a great therapist, or you could manage an adventure travel agency.

Taurus

APRIL 20-MAY 20

• • • • •

People say you're stubborn—and you are—but you're so much more than that. You are practical and reliable, with a deep inner strength that allows you to overcome just about any obstacle in your way. And in fact, you're always so prepared and realistic, that you frequently see problems coming even when they're way off in the distance. So you head them off before they even become an issue.

But for all the groundedness you naturally have as the leader of the Earth Signs, you can have wonderful flights of fancy. You love nice things and really know how to enjoy what's good in life. You're also a lot more sensitive than most people realize and can get your feelings hurt easily, especially when someone doesn't understand your good intentions.

Your favorite color tends to be green. You love music and being outdoors. And while you don't much care for change, you are loyal to the very end.

Compatibility

- **FRIENDS WITH:** You can get along with just about anybody, but you're probably closest to Virgos and Capricorns.
- **BEST FRIEND:** Your best friend is most likely to be a Water Sign, as they will smooth your rough edges and go with the flow when you're feeling a little, well, unyielding. Cancer's emotionally giving nature and natural empathy will support you when you're feeling weighted down.

Famous Taurus

ADRIENNE RICH
May 16, 1929–March 27, 2012

"To do something very common, in my own way."

You wouldn't necessarily think this, but some of the most influential and experimental writers in history have been Taureans—Karl Marx, Charlotte Brontë, Vladimir Nabokov, and William Shakespeare are all bulls. Perhaps this is because when a Taurus knows something is right, they go for it, whether or not anyone else thinks so.

Adrienne Rich is certainly no exception. This feminist poet and essayist worked not only to change public discourse on women, but on lesbian women in particular—Rich had been married and had three children, but after her husband's death she fell in love with Jamaican novelist and editor Michelle Cliff.

Rich was one of the first women to speak openly about the patriarchal nature of modern society and worked proactively against sexism. She was also a prominent anti-war and civil rights activist. In 1997 she was offered the U.S. National Medal of Arts, but she declined it in protest of the government's vote to defund the National Endowment of the Arts.

Rich continues to inspire millions of women to this day with her passion, artistry, and dedication to what she believed was right.

TAURUS CRAFT:

Illustration

You're an artist, but you're also a perfectionist. You like to know exactly what you're doing before you start. This illustration will set you up well by giving you a framework and then asking you to embellish, following your own instincts.

MATERIALS

✦ Good paper (you know how you like the finer things)

✦ Pencils, pens, paint—whatever medium works best for you

Start your illustration with the frame of your zodiac symbol:

Now, that's kind of boring, sure— but *you're* not boring. Play with it a little, offset it, stylize it. These illustrations are just examples for inspiration.

And then, embellish it. What do you love? What represents *you*? Make Taurus your own.

Events to Watch Out For

- **MOON IN TAURUS.** When you've got the moon in your sign for a couple of days, you'll likely notice your emotions getting a little out of control. It's all right, it'll pass.

- **MERCURY RETROGRADE.** Nobody likes it when Mercury is in retrograde, but you *definitely* don't. You like knowing what's going to happen and making plans, and when Mercury is wonky, it feels like your whole world is wonky.

- **MARS IN TAURUS.** This is a little tricky, as Mars is a planet of action and you like to be a little more methodical . . . So you might feel a little stagnant this month as you are pushed against your nature.

- **URANUS IN TAURUS.** Uranus spends six to seven years in a sign, and when Uranus is in Taurus, drastic things happen— sometimes good, sometimes bad. Use your judgment wisely.

Events to Look Forward To

- **SUN IN TAURUS.** You love your birthday. You don't often like being the center of attention, but a little fuss always feels good. Let yourself enjoy it.

- **MERCURY IN TAURUS.** You get along better with Mercury than most signs do. You sometimes have trouble communicating with others, and Mercury can help with that.

- **VENUS IN TAURUS.** Venus is your natural ruler, so know that you are at your very best during this time. Your creativity will flow.

- **JUPITER IN TAURUS.** You always work hard, and this is when it will start to pay off. You'll get in the groove here, and long-term plans will start to show results.

- **SATURN IN TAURUS.** After the excitement of Jupiter, this may feel a little dull, but there *is* something positive here. This is a time to clean house—both internally and externally—as you settle back down. It's good to take a breath.

Decans

VENUS DECAN
April 20–April 30

You have a lot going on, and some of it creates conflict within— you're just as stubborn as any other Taurus, but you're also more creative. You love what you like and hate what you don't like; you never do anything halfway. If you get an idea, you'll make it happen.

- **ASPECTS TO CELEBRATE.** You have a great memory and a good head on your shoulders.
- **ASPECTS TO USE WITH CAUTION.** You can be a teensy bit self-indulgent, and nobody likes getting into an argument with you.
- **POTENTIAL CAREERS.** Interior design, running a business, or starting a nonprofit.

MERCURY DECAN
May 1–May 9

Having Mercury in your court is definitely a good thing. You are great at communicating whatever it is you want to say—and it's usually something pretty important. You've got a good eye for detail, and you're just, well, hella smart.

- **ASPECTS TO CELEBRATE.** You're a great writer and speaker, and you're always thinking about something. You're very practical.
- **ASPECTS TO USE WITH CAUTION.** You can be a little distant sometimes and get impatient with overly sentimental people. Come out of your own head sometimes.
- **POTENTIAL CAREERS.** You would make a wonderful writer or editor and may want to consider journalism.

SATURN DECAN
May 10–May 20

You are so hardworking, it's a little intimidating! You're at the top of your game, always, because you put in the effort needed to stay there. You're patient and have absolute faith in your own abilities.

- **ASPECTS TO CELEBRATE.** You can literally do anything you set your mind to, and you hate procrastinating.
- **ASPECTS TO USE WITH CAUTION.** Your need for success can sometimes make you a little blind to the rest of life. Slow down and think about what really matters to you.
- **POTENTIAL CAREERS.** Um, anything? What do you want to do? You'll be amazing at it.

Gemini

MAY 21–JUNE 20

• • • • • •

It can be hard being you sometimes. You can feel like you don't quite have a handle on yourself—and with good reason! Everybody feels like they are made up of disparate parts from time to time, but you've got more of that going on than most people, as if you're literally two souls in one.

But that can be a really good thing, too. You are able to see other points of view so much better than most, and you can always keep an open mind. You're curious and full of wonder—there's so much out there in the world for you to do! You can sometimes get overwhelmed by difficult decisions, but your instincts are good. Trust them.

Your favorite color is yellow, and you always have so much energy. You're fun and never, ever boring.

Compatibility

- **FRIENDS WITH:** You have a fantastic time with Leos, Libras, and Aquarians.

- **BEST FRIEND:** Your best friend could be any of those, but you'll probably find yourself gravitating to Aries most of all. That Aries certainty will help when you feel unsure, and they have the energy to meet you where you are.

Famous Gemini

SALLY RIDE
May 26, 1951–July 23, 2012

"The stars don't look bigger,
but they do look brighter."

Sally Ride became the first American woman in space in 1983— and to this day she is still the youngest person to go to space, having ridden her explosion into the stratosphere at the tender age of thirty-two. She was also the first known LGBT astronaut, though she was very private about her personal life.

Ride was always interested in space exploration, but was also a talented tennis player and nationally ranked—she decided that science was a better long-term career. She got her start by literally answering a newspaper ad NASA ran asking for young scientists to serve as "mission specialists." Astronauts need to be outstanding both mentally and physically, and Ride was one of only five women accepted into the program that year.

Her first mission brought up all the stereotypical narrow-minded questions about being a woman going into space you might expect—"Will [space] affect your reproductive organs?" "Do you cry when things go wrong?" "What kind of makeup are you going to bring to space?" But although Ride was conscious of the symbolism of being the first woman in space, she considered herself an astronaut, period. She later said, "It's too bad this is such a big deal. It's too bad our society isn't further along."

But Ride *made* society move further along, by being able to be multiple things at once—a woman, an athlete, and a scientist.

GEMINI CRAFT:

Earrings

Being a Gemini, you can't just make one thing, you need to make two—and they shouldn't be exactly the same. This DIY project will allow you to make a pair of earrings that match, but are just different enough to feel like they're really *you*.

These are feather earrings, suitable for an Air Sign, but you can substitute beads, tassels, or whatever suits your fancy.

MATERIALS

- Feathers—you can get a pack at a craft store with a variety of sizes and colors
- Strong, fast-drying glue, like Loctite or Gorilla
- Cord ends
- Earring hooks
- Needle-nose pliers

Gather ten or so feathers, mixing and matching sizes and colors, keeping all their tips together. Dip the tips in your glue, making sure the glue covers each and every one, bonding them together.

Before the glue dries, insert the clump of glue into the cord end, making sure you're leaving the loop free to attach it to the earring hook. Take your needle-nose pliers and crimp the cord end tight, sealing it in place along with the glue.

Use your pliers to twist open the loop at the base of your earring hook. Insert the opened loop of the earring hook into the loop on the cord end, and use your pliers to close the loop of the earring hook.

And you're done! Make another earring just different enough from the first to be just right.

Events to Watch Out For

- **MERCURY IN GEMINI.** Even though Mercury is your ruling planet, a little goes a long way. Having Mercury hanging out in Gemini can make you feel even more scattered and indecisive.

- **MERCURY RETROGRADE.** You normally have no problems communicating, and so Mercury in retrograde will be a little easier on you than most—but it's still no picnic.

- **MARS IN GEMINI.** You might find yourself getting into fights during this time. They'll blow over, but try to not say anything you'll regret later.

- **URANUS IN GEMINI.** You might have a hard time focusing when Uranus first moves into Gemini. Remember, this is a seven-year journey, so keep your head down and you'll even out.

Events to Look Forward To

- **MOON IN GEMINI.** This is a time to *shine*. Get dressed up and go out—you look and feel fantastic!

- **SUN IN GEMINI.** Yay! Time to celebrate. Don't get too stressed out about making your birthday perfect—just enjoy it and have a blast.
- **VENUS IN GEMINI.** You love everyone and everything! Your enthusiastic nature is at its peak right now.
- **JUPITER IN GEMINI.** You find it so much easier to make decisions during this time. You trust your own judgment.
- **SATURN IN GEMINI.** You sometimes have a hard time accepting yourself the way you are . . . partly because, by your very nature, you change all the time! When Saturn is in Gemini, you'll feel much more at ease with yourself.

Decans

MERCURY DECAN
May 21–May 31

You have a wide range of interests, and the good news is that you're so multitalented you're probably good at all of them! You're always trying out something new, and your energy keeps you working at whatever interests you. You have a strong sense of right and wrong—and you will fight for what you believe in.

- **ASPECTS TO CELEBRATE.** You're so bright and so much fun, and you know how to bring others along with you.

- **ASPECTS TO USE WITH CAUTION.** You can get bored easily, and sometimes you get impatient with those who don't move as quickly as you do.

- **POTENTIAL CAREERS.** You might want to consider a career in the public life, maybe as a musician—you would also make a great teacher.

VENUS DECAN
June 1–June 10

People think you're really lucky—everything just seems to work out for you! But you *work* to make that happen, by trying hard, communicating well, and caring so much about what you do—and about the people around you.

- **ASPECTS TO CELEBRATE.** You're warm and fun to be around, and very generous with your time.

- **ASPECTS TO USE WITH CAUTION.** You can be a little bit impulsive, and you do tend to talk a lot.

- **POTENTIAL CAREERS.** You'd be an awesome talk show host. You're also great at public relations and marketing.

URANUS DECAN
June 11–June 20

Your friendships are very important to you. You're optimistic and think the best of people. People often come to you seeking advice, and you're always eager to not just tell them what you think. You also like to consider all sides of the situation, helping them to work out the answer for themselves.

- **ASPECTS TO CELEBRATE.** You want to make the world a better place, and you have the heart to do it.
- **ASPECTS TO USE WITH CAUTION.** You can be very persuasive without realizing it, so make sure you aren't pushing someone accidentally.
- **POTENTIAL CAREERS.** Anything in media would work really well for you, whether that's writing, podcasting, or being on-screen.

Cancer

JUNE 21–JULY 22

• • ▪ • •

The most empathetic and emotional of all the signs, you care so much about everyone, especially the people you love. You can be a little moody, particularly when someone else is experiencing some emotional upheaval—you can't help but be affected by it.

You thrive on harmony and a peaceful existence, but you are so protective and want so much to ensure the happiness of those around you, that you sometimes pick fights you can't win. You also can sometimes sacrifice your happiness for the sake of others. So you need to be careful and make sure you're looking out for *you*, too.

But your kindness and thoughtfulness go such a long way that most people absolutely love you and will never want to take advantage of you. The color white makes you feel peaceful, calming your anxieties, and you love to be near water.

Compatibility

- **FRIENDS WITH:** You love being with other Cancers, Virgos, Scorpios, and Pisces most of all, though you can get along with literally everyone.
- **BEST FRIEND:** Your best friend could be any of the above, but it may be a Taurus—they will communicate exactly what they need, which will help you feel comfortable and able to look out for yourself.

Famous Cancer

FRIDA KAHLO
July 6, 1907–July 13, 1954

"I am that clumsy human, always loving, loving, loving. And loving. And never leaving."

When she was only eighteen years old, Frida Kahlo was in a bus accident that left her body, as she described it, "broken." But her spirit was, if anything, made stronger, and she began to paint. Her work was intimate and introspective—and it was unlike that of her contemporaries. She was not appreciated by the art world of Paris, even though she was the first Mexican artist to be shown in the Louvre, and in her homeland of Mexico the art movement of the time was more focused on revolutionary works, which were often very large—murals, most of the time. While she too celebrated the Mexican indigenous culture like the muralists did, she came at it from a different perspective, focusing more on folk art and identity.

She had a tumultuous relationship with fellow artist Diego Rivera and pushed back against artists who tried to categorize her. French artist and founder of surrealism André Bréton called her a surrealist—but she denied it, saying "I never painted my dreams. I painted my own reality." Kahlo's deeply felt emotions propelled her artistic expressions, and she worked through her ongoing struggles with physical pain and emotional upheaval by painting self-portraits again and again, exploring and questioning the idea of the self. She never let anyone tell her who she was, but constantly echoed back and forth between what she saw in others and what they saw in her.

CANCER CRAFT:

Worry Stone

You tend to worry sometimes, and this craft can help you make something with intention—this stone can be a place where you ground yourself and allow your worries to rest so that you can go about your day.

MATERIALS

- A smooth, round stone
- Hot water
- Soap
- Rubbing alcohol
- Sharpie or other permanent marker
- Baking sheet
- Aluminum foil
- Oven mitt

Get a smooth, round stone. This can be something you purchase at a craft store, but it can also be fun to go out to a river and look for an appropriate rock. You want something relatively flat, but with enough heft to fit comfortably in your hand.

When you've found the right stone, make sure it's clean—scrub it with hot water and soap, and then wipe it down with rubbing alcohol to make extra sure you've got all the dirt off.

Take a Sharpie or other permanent marker in whatever color you like—if you have a dark stone, you might use white or silver—and draw something on the stone. You can draw your constellation:

Or you could use your zodiac symbol:

Or you could write something else entirely—it's up to you!

Line a baking sheet with foil, and bake your stone at 200 degrees for thirty minutes or so. Carefully remove it from the oven, then let it cool entirely before touching!

Events to Watch Out For

- **MOON IN CANCER.** This isn't really a bad time; it's just a quiet time. The moon makes you even more emotional than usual, and you kind of just want to snuggle up in bed, staying warm and cozy. Let yourself do that.

- **MERCURY RETROGRADE.** You handle this better than most because you are more able to intuit what's going on when things aren't working . . . But others will be having a hard time, and that's hard on you.

- **VENUS IN CANCER.** So many feelings! So much love! This can be a very good time, or it can be a very overwhelming time.

- **SATURN IN CANCER.** This time might be a little frustrating for you, as your intuition will be blocked a little bit by Saturn's practicality.

- **URANUS IN CANCER.** Uranus is very forward-thinking, and you like to pay the most attention to what is close to you. Again, this isn't a bad thing—it could be very good! But it may require you to stretch a little. You'll have Uranus pushing you along for seven years, and you can get a lot done in that time.

Events to Look Forward To

- **SUN IN CANCER.** It can be hard to have everyone focusing their attention on you when you're so used to *giving* attention—but enjoy it! It's because they love you.
- **MERCURY IN CANCER.** You are able to communicate so well with everyone right now!
- **MARS IN CANCER.** You're always nice—unless someone steps on someone you love—but you'll be particularly happy during this time, because everybody else will be nicer, too.
- **JUPITER IN CANCER.** You are normally ruled by your emotions, but Jupiter's logic will help ground you during this time.

Decans

MOON DECAN
June 21–June 30

You have so much heart and want to do so much for others . . . so sometimes you can have a hard time saying no when you really should. Your ability to *feel* so much is what makes you such a kind person, even if you can be a bit sensitive.

- **ASPECTS TO CELEBRATE.** You can intuit so much of what someone else is feeling, and you show love with all your heart.
- **ASPECTS TO USE WITH CAUTION.** You have a quick temper, particularly when your feelings get hurt.
- **POTENTIAL CAREERS.** You love *doing* things for people, so you might want to consider opening a bakery or restaurant.

MARS DECAN
July 1–July 12

Having a little Mars energy in your corner will make you a little more aggressive—which may make you get into fights more often, but will also make sure you remember to put yourself first sometimes and ask for what you need.

- **ASPECTS TO CELEBRATE.** You're just as kind as any other Cancer, but you have an added thoughtfulness that makes you see things more clearly.
- **ASPECTS TO USE WITH CAUTION.** You have some trouble forgiving those who have hurt you.
- **POTENTIAL CAREERS.** Given your thoughtful empathy and your ability to hold a boundary, you would make a good therapist or counselor.

NEPTUNE DECAN

July 13–July 22

You're open and adaptable. You can basically show up for those you care about however they need you to. You've got a powerful imagination and are very creative.

- **ASPECTS TO CELEBRATE.** You love to keep things close—your best friends and your family matter more to you than just about anything, and you make sure they know it.
- **ASPECTS TO USE WITH CAUTION.** You can be a little shy, and you don't handle stress very well.
- **POTENTIAL CAREERS.** You love things that have history attached to them, so you would be a great museum curator or art dealer.

Leo

JULY 23–AUGUST 22

• • • • •

Y ou are a natural-born leader. You have a big personality and love being the center of attention—which is great, because most people really, really like you! You're confident and creative, and your sense of humor makes it easier for you to bring people together, even when they're all really different.

You are dramatic . . . but you're not a drama queen, because you're pretty self-aware and genuinely want to do your best and *be* your best. You're a natural problem-solver, and you're very loyal. Your emotions run high, and you love fiercely. You bring out the best in everyone around you.

You love the sun and being outdoors, and you look great in orange. You work very hard, and you are generous in lots of different ways—you love to give gifts (and you love to receive them, too!) and are also always ready to give your time and energy to anyone who needs your warm support.

Compatibility

- **FRIENDS WITH:** You're compatible with more different kinds of people with most signs, but you get along really well with other Leos, Aries, Geminis, and Libras.

- **BEST FRIEND:** Your best friend is likely to come from just about anywhere, as you see the good is most people—and they see the good in you—but you and Sagittarius get along *great*. You both have a ton of energy, are optimistic, and love to have a great time. Your imaginations explode together.

Famous Leo

FATIMA JINNAH
July 30, 1893–July 9, 1967

*"There is a magic power
in your own hands."*

Fatima Jinnah is known as the Mother of Pakistan. In 1947, what had been British-occupied India was divided into two nations: now known as India and Pakistan. Jinnah's brother Muhammad Ali Jinnah was Pakistan's first governor general, and together with a number of other politicians and revolutionaries, they created a country for their people.

Jinnah cofounded the Pakistan's Women's Association, helping to settle female migrants in the new country. She fought for the rights of women, for democracy, and for the rights of the Pakistani people. Unfortunately, after her brother's death, Muhammad Ayub Khan seized the presidency of Pakistan and turned the country into a military dictatorship. Jinnah left public life, had her written work censored, and was prevented from continuing her work for equal rights.

But toward the end of her life, she returned to the political stage to run for president against Ayub Khan. The election was rigged, unsurprisingly, but despite Khan's interference, she won two of Pakistan's largest cities. She died two years later, with nearly half a million people attending her funeral in the city of Karachi. She remains one of the most honored leaders of Pakistan.

LEO CRAFT:

Suncatcher

The sun is your power source, and you adore each other. Celebrate that relationship with this suncatcher.

MATERIALS

+ Scissors
+ Clear contact paper
+ Wooden embroidery hoop

+ A collection of orange leaves, flowers, tissue paper— whatever strikes your fancy! Play with a color and texture palette that inspires your creativity.
+ Hemp string

Start by cutting your contact paper to fit inside your embroidery hoop. You'll want to make it a half inch or so wider in circumference—don't worry, you'll trim it later.

Pull the paper backing off the contact paper. Arrange your leaves, flowers, and tissue paper artfully on the sticky paper. Once you've finished, press a second piece of contact paper in place, pushing the leaves flat and squeezing out any air bubbles.

Open up the embroidery hoop and insert your pressed contact papers. The edges will spill up over the sides of the hoop as you lock it in place. Trim any overlap with scissors.

Use hemp string to hang your suncatcher in the window.

Events to Watch Out For

• **MERCURY RETROGRADE.** You'll get frustrated easily during this time—you don't have patience for the miscommunications that often come up when Mercury goes haywire!

• **MARS IN LEO.** You've got quite a roar there, Lion—you'll want to see if you can tamp it down during this time, as your temper may get the better of you.

- **JUPITER IN LEO.** So you know how you have a little bit of an ego sometimes? You'll want to watch that now.
- **SATURN IN LEO.** Saturn brings structure to your life, a certain kind of order . . . and you're likely to feel hemmed in. You like vibrancy and motion and passion, and that's just not Saturn's vibe.
- **URANUS IN LEO.** You can get a little demanding during this time—take a breath and remember how happy you are when you're making other people happy. That said, Uranus may give you the push you need over this length of time to help you achieve all that you dream of.

Events to Look Forward To

- **MOON IN LEO.** While this is a time for introspection, it's a *fun* kind of introspection—there's still energy here, and it's a time when your emotions are active in a good way.
- **SUN IN LEO.** This isn't just your birthday—this is you and the sun hanging out together *all month*. This is peak you.
- **MERCURY IN LEO.** This is a great time to speak your mind—because you will be speaking from the heart and everyone will know it.
- **VENUS IN LEO.** You have so much love—get it out there!

Decans

SUN DECAN
July 23–August 2

Leo, you're always a little bit extra . . . And, well, that's even truer here! You are *fiercely* yourself, with all the creativity, power, charm, and passion that entails.

- **ASPECTS TO CELEBRATE.** You have a gigantic heart. You love big, and you show it. You bring so much energy to your own life— and to the lives of those around you.
- **ASPECTS TO USE WITH CAUTION.** You are proud of

yourself—justifiably! But don't let it turn into arrogance.

- **POTENTIAL CAREERS.** You will *shine* wherever you are—so where do you want to be? Onstage? On-screen? On the radio?

JUPITER DECAN
August 3–August 12

If you've always felt like you're not *really* a Leo, this is why—Jupiter heavily counteracts some of Leo's most famous tendencies. You don't necessarily like being the center of attention, and you're a lot less extroverted than most Leos. Those qualities are replaced by being very thoughtful and direct.

- **ASPECTS TO CELEBRATE.** You value honesty very highly, and you practice what you preach. You work well under pressure and rise to meet challenges.

- **ASPECTS TO USE WITH CAUTION.** You are less optimistic than your typical Leo and can be a little anxious sometimes.

- **POTENTIAL CAREERS.** You would be a great teacher or a great agent. You may also want to consider a career in marketing.

MARS DECAN
August 13–August 22

You are extremely driven and so passionate about what you want that you are pretty much guaranteed to get it—after all, you work hard enough for it! You love learning, and you have a wonderfully curious nature.

- **ASPECTS TO CELEBRATE.** You're a great listener, because you really want to know and understand what's going on with someone else—and because you care deeply.

- **ASPECTS TO USE WITH CAUTION.** You don't handle disappointment well.

- **POTENTIAL CAREERS.** You would be a terrific lawyer or anything that asks you to advocate on behalf of someone else.

Virgo

AUGUST 23–SEPTEMBER 22

• • ● ● • •

You're thoughtful and careful, and you take a methodical approach to life. You may seem overly serious, but in fact you care deeply about others and have such a big heart. You are quite private though, and so maybe you don't demonstrate those feelings as openly as other signs do.

You show how much you care by thinking about what others need and how everything will work well. You are very detail-oriented and can get a little caught up running in circles if no one else is sweating the small stuff—you know that there is no such thing! That said, you've got Mercury as your ruling planet, so you are able to communicate so well with others that you can get everyone on board with your approach.

You like muted colors like lavenders and grays, maybe with a soft brown. These gentle colors help you see more clearly what really matters; you prefer not to be distracted by too much drama.

Compatibility

- **FRIENDS WITH:** You get along well with Tauruses, Cancers, and Capricorns—they all relate well with you and appreciate the things that are important to you.
- **BEST FRIEND:** Scorpios will get you like nobody else. They are able to look deep, so they'll understand and see what you're feeling without you having to make a big deal about it. You also both value your alone time—which makes you appreciate each other all the more.

Famous Virgo

QUEEN ELIZABETH I
September 7, 1533–March 24, 1603

"I know I have the body of a weak and feeble woman,
but I have the heart and stomach of a king,
and of a king of England, too."

It is impossible not to feature the Virgin Queen as the epitome of all Virgos—but not because of her supposed virginity. No, if ever there was a person who was cautious, thoughtful, and attentive to detail, it was Elizabeth I. It was unlikely enough that she would ever gain the throne, much less hold it with success—she was the daughter of Henry VIII and Anne Boleyn, whose head he had chopped off. Elizabeth was then declared illegitimate and only managed to gain the throne after her half-sister Mary I died. Mary was the first queen of England, in fact, but her rule was short-lived and contested.

Elizabeth learned from her mistakes. Whoever married the queen would become the king and therefore would rule England, and Elizabeth wasn't having that. She engaged in a series of political courtships, but never married. Instead, she ruled herself, keeping England out of wars when possible and leading the country to one of the greatest military victories in English history—the defeat of the Spanish Armada.

Elizabeth ruled for forty-four years, and during that time, England prospered. Art flourished, as William Shakespeare, Christopher Marlowe, Edmund Spenser, and other poets and playwrights of the time became popular both with the nobility and the people. Elizabeth stood as a strong woman in a time when no one believed such a person could exist.

VIRGO CRAFT:

Lip Balm

Mercury is your ruling planet, so you're a strong communicator—and this lip balm will help you remember that.

MATERIALS

✦ 1–2 tsp beeswax pellets

✦ 2 tsp coconut oil

✦ 2 tsp shea butter

✦ Leftover lipstick (optional)

✦ Vanilla extract or other flavoring (optional)

✦ Small jar or tin

Melt your beeswax, coconut oil, and shea butter over very low heat. If your house gets quite hot, add the larger amount of beeswax; if it stays cool even in the summer, you'll be fine with just one teaspoon. Stir until the oils are well blended.

Remove from the heat and stir in your leftover lipstick if you want to add a tint to your lip balm, and one-eighth teaspoon of vanilla extract or other flavoring if you want to have a slightly scented or flavored lip balm.

Pour into your tin and allow your lip balm to cool completely.

Events to Watch Out For

- **MERCURY IN VIRGO.** Your mind is sharper than ever, and you become very productive. Just make sure to take it easy sometimes and not be overly critical—especially of yourself.

- **MERCURY RETROGRADE.** You do *not* like this time. Everything is going haywire, and it's making you crazy. Take deep breaths.

- **VENUS IN VIRGO.** This isn't a *bad* time, necessarily—but it can be tricky. This is when you're really examining your own emotions and the ways you relate to people.

- **JUPITER IN VIRGO.** This is another time when you might be a little overly critical of yourself and others.

Events to Look Forward To

- **MOON IN VIRGO.** This is a time to do some reorganizing and tidying up—all things that you like!
- **SUN IN VIRGO.** You have a lot of energy during your birthday month, and that's fantastic! Let loose and enjoy yourself.
- **SATURN IN VIRGO.** Oh, you're so happy right now! Everything is organized and practical and totally in order.

Decans

MERCURY DECAN
August 23–September 2

You are really smart, and you put your intelligence to good use. You work hard at the things that are important to you, and you make sure that everything you do is done well.

- **ASPECTS TO CELEBRATE.** You put so much thought into what you do that you can reach a deeper understanding of a topic than just about anybody else.

- **ASPECTS TO USE WITH CAUTION.** You can get a little caught up with work—let loose and have fun sometimes!

- **POTENTIAL CAREERS.** You like to go *deep,* so you may end up being a scientist or a researcher—something that allows you to pursue your interests to their fullest.

SATURN DECAN
September 3–September 12

Combine Saturn's determination and organization with Mercury's communication skills, and you have a pretty formidable person. You have a sly, sarcastic sense of humor and a small, select group of friends you love dearly.

- **ASPECTS TO CELEBRATE.** You love puzzles and games and are always coming up with fun and unusual activities.

- **ASPECTS TO USE WITH CAUTION.** You can burn out if you aren't careful—make sure you don't put all of your energy into something that just isn't going to come into being.

- **POTENTIAL CAREERS.** You love knowing how things work and figuring out what's going on. You would be a great journalist or detective.

VENUS DECAN

September 13–September 22

You have a fabulous can-do mentality—and if something needs doing, you're the one to handle it. You can manage just about anything that gets thrown your way. You're optimistic and caring.

- **ASPECTS TO CELEBRATE.** You are warmhearted and generous, and you will protect those you care about.
- **ASPECTS TO USE WITH CAUTION.** You don't necessarily like being told what you should do—you trust your own instincts.
- **POTENTIAL CAREERS.** You're a natural writer, and have a good imagination, too—so you may want to be a novelist or a screenwriter.

Libra

SEPTEMBER 23–OCTOBER 22

•• ••••

As a Libra, you love balance. You want everything to be fair and just, but you also want to know that your world is filled with *everything* and you're not missing out on any part of life's experience. You love to be surrounded by others—though you don't like conflict and will do just about anything to avoid it. But when conflict does arise between others, you're a great mediator, able to see all sides and help people who are disagreeing understand another point of view.

You are very curious, especially about human nature. You often sit and observe what's going on around you, and when you do speak up, you have a level of insight that most other signs don't. Your instinct will always be to put others before yourself, so make sure you're surrounding yourself with good people who won't take advantage of your thoughtfulness.

Your favorite color is a peaceful blue, and you have a calm but vivid imagination. You have a lot of self-awareness and are always seeking to understand yourself and others better.

Compatibility

- **FRIENDS WITH:** You love everybody, but you have a great time with Geminis, Leos, and Sagittarians, as they are all fun-loving.
- **BEST FRIEND:** Your best friend may well be an Aquarius. You both have a rich inner life and think deeply about things. You'll have an easy time with each other.

Famous Libra

SERENA WILLIAMS
born September 26, 1981

"The success of every woman should be the inspiration to another. We should raise each other up. Make sure you're very courageous: be strong, be extremely kind, and above all be humble."

Serena Williams has, to date, won more Grand Slam singles titles than anyone else in the world—man or woman. She and her sister Venus learned tennis on the public courts of Los Angeles with their father—you would think their competitiveness and athleticism would give them a troubled relationship, but it hasn't appeared to be the case. They team up for doubles tournaments and support each other like no one else.

Williams's style is aggressive and fast—and her serve is often described as the best in the history of women's tennis. She has overcome a variety of injuries, returning as champion—and, in

2020, she returned from maternity leave and won yet another singles title.

Williams has proven again and again that she is tough as nails, but she has done something more than that for women in sports—she has set an example of femininity combined with athleticism. She has also been an activist for Black Lives Matter and a supporter of the LGBT community.

LIBRA CRAFT:

Tie-Dye

This look is surprisingly versatile, and you can adapt it to whatever style you're rocking these days. You don't have to use Kool-Aid—a tie-dye kit or any other kind of fabric dye will work just as well!

MATERIALS

- Kool-Aid packet, unsweetened (you might consider Berry Blue or Blue Raspberry)
- Bowl
- 1 cup white vinegar
- Pencil
- Plain white shirt
- Rubber bands
- Plastic gloves
- Plastic bag

Empty the packet of Kool-Aid into a bowl, and stir in the white vinegar.

Using a pencil, mark out the points of your constellation on the front of your shirt. Make it as large as you can, as you'll need as much fabric as possible. At each point, pinch a bit of your shirt—anywhere is fine—and twist it into a spiral, turning as tight as you can. Secure it with a rubber band. Each one will create a spiral.

Dip your shirt into the bowl of Kool-Aid. Push it down with your hands (make sure you're wearing those gloves!) and let the dye soak through. Let it sit for an hour, then remove your shirt and place it in a plastic bag. Let it sit for twenty-four hours, and then rinse it in hot water until the water runs clear. At this point you can undo the rubber bands and let your shirt dry. You may want to wash it before wearing it if it still smells like vinegar, but make sure you wash it with like colors, as it will bleed for the first few washes.

Events to Watch Out For

- **MOON IN LIBRA.** Most of the time you like being in a crowd, but this is a time to hunker down with your bestie. Be a reflection for each other.
- **MERCURY RETROGRADE.** All right, everything's going haywire. Your sense of fairness helps you recognize that it affects everybody equally, and you know that this too shall pass.

- **MARS IN LIBRA.** This isn't your natural state. You'll find yourself being a little confrontational—which is just not your style. But don't worry, it's okay to set a few boundaries during this time.

- **JUPITER IN LIBRA.** You want everything to be fair and just, and Jupiter accentuates that feeling. But the problem is, things don't always work out that way. Don't let it get you down.

Events to Look Forward To

- **SUN IN LIBRA.** It's rare that you get to be in the spotlight—and the thing is, you enjoy it as much as anybody else! You're always watching out for others—let them watch out for you on your birthday month.

- **MERCURY IN LIBRA.** You'll have an easier time than ever helping everybody get along—people always listen to you, but right now they listen even more closely.

- **VENUS IN LIBRA.** Venus is your planet, and so having her hanging out in your sign can make you feel things more deeply than usual—especially the love you have for everyone around you.

- **SATURN IN LIBRA.** You are naturally attentive and observant, and Saturn boosts these qualities in you.

Decans

VENUS DECAN
September 23–October 2

Your loving nature is what makes you want to ensure that everyone is happy and that everything is right with the world. You know how to make everyone around you feel loved and can spread your attention and warmth throughout a crowd.

- **ASPECTS TO CELEBRATE.** You're never judgmental and always listen and react with kindness.
- **ASPECTS TO USE WITH CAUTION.** You can be a little naive and gullible, and not-so-nice people could take advantage of you.
- **POTENTIAL CAREERS.** You would make a great publicist or therapist—and you would also be great at event planning.

URANUS DECAN
October 3–October 13

You could easily be a social justice warrior. You think deeply about things, particularly about interpersonal relations, and you have a strong sense of what is *right*.

- **ASPECTS TO CELEBRATE.** You're optimistic and have a ton of great ideas, and you work hard to put them to use.
- **ASPECTS TO USE WITH CAUTION.** You do so much for others, but you have a hard time asking for help when you need it.
- **POTENTIAL CAREERS.** You might want to consider working for a nonprofit, leading group counseling, or becoming a mediator.

MERCURY DECAN
October 14–October 22

You can convince just about anybody of just about anything—but you always use your powers for good. You are at ease with strangers and can manage difficult situations, making sure that everybody reaches the best possible solution.

- **ASPECTS TO CELEBRATE.** You make decisions carefully, taking into account what your mind and your heart tell you is right.
- **ASPECTS TO USE WITH CAUTION.** You often take on too much responsibility, because you're good at it. Let someone else carry the load sometimes.
- **POTENTIAL CAREERS.** You would be a great team manager or head of human resources.

Scorpio

OCTOBER 23–NOVEMBER 21

• • • • • •

Y ou're a Water Sign, so you're quite emotional—but not in the same way other Water Signs are. Your emotions make you passionate, and they are what drive you. You feel so strongly about things, and you work hard for what you care about.

But while you know how you feel, you don't necessarily like to talk about your feelings with other people. You're a very private person, and you don't trust easily. This is partly because you always show up as *yourself*, 100%, and you judge other people when they aren't completely genuine.

You're honest to a fault, but never cruel, as you have a deep sense of empathy. Remember that empathy when people don't quite meet your expectations, and do your best not to retreat into your shell.

Your favorite color is a deep red, to represent just how much and how deeply you love.

Compatibility

- **FRIENDS WITH:** You get along well with Cancers and Pisces, your fellow Water Signs, who understand how deeply your emotions run. You'll also get along well with Tauruses and Capricorns, whose sense of right and wrong will resonate well with you.

- **BEST FRIEND:** But Virgo is likely to be someone you can truly rely on, someone you can share your deepest self with. You know and trust each other.

Famous Scorpio

MARIE CURIE
November 7, 1867–July 4, 1934

*"I am among those who think
that science has great beauty."*

Marie Curie was the first woman to win a Nobel Prize. She was the first person, man or woman, to win two, and the only person to date who has won a Nobel Prize in two different fields of science—physics and chemistry.

Curie and her husband Pierre worked together, funding their research themselves through teaching. They didn't have a high-tech lab or much of any support at all—they worked out of a converted shed that leaked in the rain. But they wanted to help people. The recent discovery of radioactivity—a term Marie Curie coined—and its potential uses—for example, x-rays and cancer treatments—inspired them to discover and isolate new elements, including polonium and radium. Marie Curie found radium based on her work alone.

She advocated for radium's use in the field during World War I, as it allowed operations to be carried out more quickly. It's estimated that over a million wounded soldiers were treated thanks to her efforts. She also attempted to donate her gold Nobel Prize to the war effort but was refused. So she gave them her prize money instead.

Prizes didn't matter to her. People and her work did. In fact, she spent so much time on her research that she contracted aplastic anemia, a deficiency of blood cells caused by long-term exposure to radiation.

SCORPIO CRAFT:

Strawberry DNA

In honor of Madame Curie, let's get our science on, shall we? It is possible—in fact, it's very easy—to extract strands of DNA from strawberries! They're particularly good for this because they yield a lot of DNA and have eight copies of each chromosome, making their DNA larger and easier to see.

MATERIALS

- Isopropyl alcohol (91%)
- Water
- Clear glass
- Dish soap
- Salt
- Ziplock bag
- Strawberry
- Strainer
- Tweezers

Put the bottle of isopropyl alcohol in the freezer. This will stop the DNA from dissolving when the time comes.

Add six tablespoons water to your glass, then stir in two teaspoons of dish soap. Stir gently so it doesn't get all foamy. Stir in one-quarter teaspoon salt, again gently, until the salt dissolves. This solution will extract the DNA from the strawberry! The soap will help dissolve the strawberry's cell membranes, and the salt will break up the protein chains that hold the nucleic acids together. Pour it into a Ziplock bag and add your strawberry (remove the green leaves first). Squeeze out as much air as you can and close the bag.

Now, mash away! Squish up that strawberry, breaking it down as much as you can.

Rinse out your glass and strain the strawberry mixture into it. Add one teaspoon of chilled isopropyl alcohol. The mixture will begin to separate, with a layer of white on top. That white stuff is the DNA! You can pull it out carefully with your tweezers.

Events to Watch Out For

- **MOON IN SCORPIO.** You're used to having a lot of feelings, and you're pretty good at managing them. But when the moon is pulling at you, this can be more difficult, and you may feel overwhelmed by emotions.

- **MERCURY RETROGRADE.** You're not the best communicator under the best of circumstances—so this will be an especially difficult time for you. Try extra hard to be open and patient.

- **MARS IN SCORPIO.** You're not normally confrontational, but you do have trouble being forgiving. With Mars energy floating around, you're likely to get into more battles. Pick them carefully.

- **SATURN IN SCORPIO.** You can get a little single-minded when Saturn is around. Try to take some breaks and get out and have fun.

Events to Look Forward To

- **SUN IN SCORPIO.** You don't *love* attention most of the time . . . but it's okay to let loose and allow yourself to bask in it just for a little while. It's your birthday, enjoy it!

- **MERCURY IN SCORPIO.** You will find it so much easier to talk about the things you normally want to skip past.

- **VENUS IN SCORPIO.** You are naturally passionate, and having Venus around will only make you more so!

- **JUPITER IN SCORPIO.** You have a strong sense of right and wrong, and you trust your instincts. Jupiter will make those instincts even clearer.

Decans

MARS DECAN

October 23–November 2

You are a deeply mysterious person to everyone except yourself. You have a great sense of self-knowledge and self-awareness; you just don't necessarily need to share everything with everyone.

- **ASPECTS TO CELEBRATE.** You are magnetic—people are drawn to your passion and energy.
- **ASPECTS TO USE WITH CAUTION.** You can be a little too secretive, and your strong feelings sometimes make you a little unforgiving.
- **POTENTIAL CAREERS.** Your thoughtful, outside-the-box approach would make you a great engineer or doctor.

JUPITER DECAN

November 3–November 11

You are intelligent and ambitious and want to do great things in the world—and you have the commitment and creativity to achieve results.

- **ASPECTS TO CELEBRATE.** You're generous and artistic and can have a powerful impact on those around you.
- **ASPECTS TO USE WITH CAUTION.** You can get a little distracted and caught up in various projects. Remember to pay attention to your friends and loved ones.
- **POTENTIAL CAREERS.** You'll do great at whatever it is you want to do, but you may want to focus on a career in science or the arts.

MOON DECAN
November 12–November 21

You feel things deeply, and you have an incredible sense of empathy. Like all Scorpios, you're quite private, but when the right people get close to you, you will have a strong and deep relationship.

- **ASPECTS TO CELEBRATE.** You are sensitive and work hard to make those around you happy.
- **ASPECTS TO USE WITH CAUTION.** You can get your feelings hurt pretty easily, and when that happens, you tend to lash out.
- **POTENTIAL CAREERS.** You would be an amazing therapist or editor.

Sagittarius

NOVEMBER 22–DECEMBER 21

• • • • • •

You have so much curiosity and joy in life. You make the world around you sparkle. You're optimistic and enthusiastic, and you give fantastic hugs. Like all Fire Signs, you want to experience *everything* and are driven by a deep desire to know and understand the world around you.

You are hilarious and have a fantastic imagination. Your friends love to hang out with you, because you can find the fun in absolutely anything. But you are also deeply caring and empathetic and will pour your soul into helping someone in need.

You're not always amazing at following the rules, because you get so caught up in what interests you that you have a hard time settling down and focusing. But your genuine desire to learn and to please helps you through.

Your favorite color is purple—you like to see and be seen! You have a definite sense of style, and it's all your own.

Compatibility

- **FRIENDS WITH:** Everybody likes you, and you like just about everybody back. But you'll have a great time with the signs Aries, Libra, and Aquarius, because they share your outgoing, fun-loving nature.
- **BEST FRIEND:** You and Leo get each other like no one else. You're both passionate and imaginative, and both have a fiery nature that is optimistic rather than argumentative. You'll go on a lot of adventures together.

Famous Sagittarius

ADA LOVELACE
December 10, 1815–November 27, 1852

"Understand well as I may, my comprehension can only be an infinitesimal fraction of all I want to understand."

Ada Lovelace was the daughter of the famous poet Lord Byron, though she never really knew him—he left her and her mother when she was just a few weeks old. And yet in some ways, she followed in her father's footsteps, for she too was drawn to and wanted to understand the beauty of the world . . . only for her, that curiosity expressed itself through science.

Her mother insisted that she be taught mathematics and science, hoping to drill out any poetical tendencies she might have inherited from her father. She was so well-versed in both that as a teenager she formed what would come to be a long working relationship with mathematician Charles Babbage, the man who is known as the "father of computers." Babbage had recently invented the Analytical Engine, which was in essence a simple computer.

Lovelace was fascinated by it. She thought deeply about how to put it to greater use, as Babbage's invention was capable only of simple mathematics. In the notes of an article she was working on, Lovelace wrote what may well have been the world's first computer program, a series of instructions to make the machine do something other than what it was originally planned to do.

But more importantly, Lovelace had vision. Babbage and everyone else thought of computers as nothing more than calculators, but Lovelace really delved into what computers might come to mean and how they could change the human experience. She called this kind of approach "poetical science."

SAGITTARIUS CRAFT:
Vision Board

This project is a supercool DIY bulletin board. Once it's set up, you can hang anything you like on it, from interesting things you find in the woods or pictures of you and your friends to poems or even pictures from magazines—anything!

MATERIALS

- ½-inch thick plywood, 2 feet by 3 feet
- Paintbrush
- Silver metallic paint
- Pencil
- Tape measure
- Hammer
- 16 decorative copper nails
- Pliers
- 18-gauge copper jewelry wire
- Scissors
- Mini clothespins

Paint the top and edges of the plywood with your metallic paint. It may take a couple of coats. Let it dry completely.

Take a pencil, and lightly mark where you want your nails to go. You want them evenly spaced along the edges of the plywood, about one inch in from the edge. You'll have three across the top and bottom and four down each of the sides—use your measuring tape to get the distance right. Once you're sure you've got them right, go ahead and hammer them in.

Using your pliers, twist the copper wire around the top left nail, securing it in place. String it all the way down to the bottom left nail, keeping it very taut. Use the pliers to secure it, then cut. Repeat across the top nails, until you have three vertical lines of wire going up and down your board.

Repeat the same process horizontally, until you have four horizontal lines of wire above the vertical wires.

Use the last two copper nails on the back of the vision board to hook up a wire to hang it on your wall. You may need to twist or braid the copper wire to strengthen it.

Use the mini clothespins to fill your board with inspiration and fun!

Events to Watch Out For

- **MOON IN SAGITTARIUS.** You are even more impulsive than usual right now, as you long to go on an adventure. That's great, but take care and use your head.

- **MERCURY IN SAGITTARIUS.** You're pretty talkative most of the time . . . keep an eye on that tendency now, as you may not realize you are dominating the conversation.

- **MERCURY RETROGRADE.** You'll be frustrated and feel like you're not being heard. Make a special effort to be patient.

- **MARS IN SAGITTARIUS.** You might be a little more impulsive than usual at this time. Check yourself if you need to.

- **SATURN IN SAGITTARIUS.** This isn't a bad time by any means, just a little less fun than you're used to. You'll be thoughtful, instead.

Events to Look Forward To

- **SUN IN SAGITTARIUS.** You sometimes have a hard time on your birthday because you set your expectations so high. Let yourself just have a good time, and everyone else will, too!

- **VENUS IN SAGITTARIUS.** Dole out those hugs! You're always pretty good at letting people know how much you love them, but you'll feel an even greater surge of affection.

- **JUPITER IN SAGITTARIUS.** This is a wonderful time to dive into a project or a new subject. Go deep!

Decans

JUPITER DECAN
November 22–December 2

You are just so much fun. You're enthusiastic and bubbly, and you're always coming up with great ideas. You're friends with absolutely everyone, though only a few select people are trusted with your deepest feelings.

- **ASPECTS TO CELEBRATE.** Your spontaneity will bring you all the amazing experiences you crave, as you enjoy the heck out of life.
- **ASPECTS TO USE WITH CAUTION.** You can be pretty competitive.
- **POTENTIAL CAREERS.** You would be an amazing coach or travel writer.

MARS DECAN
December 3–December 11

You combine a sense of adventure with the bravery of Mars . . . which sounds like it might lead you into dangerous situations. Fortunately you have terrific instincts, and everything always works out.

- **ASPECTS TO CELEBRATE.** You are very kind, independent, and work hard for the things you care about.
- **ASPECTS TO USE WITH CAUTION.** You can get discouraged easily, though you don't often show it. Let people in so they can help you!
- **POTENTIAL CAREERS.** You'd be a great social activist or maybe a martial arts or dance teacher.

LEO DECAN
December 12–December 21

You are thoughtful and generous and want so much to make everyone around you happy—and you usually succeed! You love to laugh, and people love to laugh with you.

- **ASPECTS TO CELEBRATE.** You are passionate and adventurous and are drawn to everything magical.
- **ASPECTS TO USE WITH CAUTION.** You can be fairly impulsive, so make an effort to think things through.
- **POTENTIAL CAREERS.** You could be anything from a stand-up comic to a yoga teacher to a scientist.

Capricorn

DECEMBER 22–JANUARY 19

• • • • • •

Y ou are very independent and can be quite serious—but that's just because you know what's important to you. You can be a little hard to get to know, because you can be quite private about what's going on inside your head. But once someone manages to break down your walls, they have a friend for life. You are loyal and always there when your friends need you, and though you do like to keep your boundaries, when you let loose everyone has a great time.

You're ambitious and want to make the most out of your life—so you work hard and study hard. You are harder on yourself than on anyone else and blame yourself for your mistakes . . . although you always learn from them. You crave structure and predictability, and so you plan very carefully. Along those lines, you love traditions! The holidays are one of your favorite times of year, and you have a great time creating fun pastimes for you and your friends to come back to again and again.

You have a clear sense of your own style, and you look great in brown and black.

Compatibility

- **FRIENDS WITH:** Earth Signs tend to get along with one another, as they have a shared outlook on life, so Tauruses, Virgos, and other Capricorns will likely be close friends. Scorpios will respect your sense of privacy, and you will be at ease with one another.
- **BEST FRIEND:** But the person who will truly bring you out of your shell is probably a Pisces. Their caring and sensitive nature will help you feel safe expressing your true self and complement your more practical side.

Famous Capricorn

MADAM C.J. WALKER
December 23, 1867–May 25, 1919

"I got my start by giving myself a start."

Born Sarah Breedlove, Madam C.J. Walker was likely America's first female self-made millionaire. She was also the first Black female millionaire. Her parents were recently freed slaves—Sarah was the first member of her family born free. And yet, in her early childhood she did housework and picked cotton, because nothing much had changed yet for Black people in the United States.

Madam C.J. Walker was one of the forces that started that change. When she was in her thirties, she developed a scalp condition that caused her to lose much of her hair, probably because of her work as a laundress and her exposure to toxic chemicals. She began working for a hair care company that offered products specific to Black women, but eventually developed her own line of products. The "Walker System" of hair care actually revolutionized the industry, and Madam C.J. Walker eventually had a small army of salespeople known as Walker Agents, empowering other Black women to make a living.

As her success grew, Madam C.J. Walker became determined to bring that kind of success to more men and women like her, joining the executive committee of the newly established National Association for the Advancement of Colored People and donating more money to them than they had ever received before. At her death, her will dictated that two-thirds of her estate go to charity.

CAPRICORN CRAFT:

Clay Pot

Tap into your Earth Sign nature with this clay pot. You can use it to store jewelry or thumbtacks or as a vase.

MATERIALS

✦ Air-dry clay
✦ Knife
✦ Small water glass

✦ Toothpick
✦ Paintbrush
✦ Acrylic paint

Roll out your clay into a sheet about a quarter inch thick. Use your knife and water glass to cut out a circle to serve as the base of the pot. Next, cut out a rectangle to serve as the body of the pot—make it a little longer than you think you'll need, just in case, and about two to two and a half inches wide.

Wrap the rectangle around the circle, trimming it as necessary. Press the circle into the rectangle to join them together, then smooth the edges.

Use your toothpick to draw your astrological sign or your constellation—your choice! Paint the pot as desired, then allow it to dry completely.

Events to Watch Out For

- **MERCURY RETROGRADE.** You can actually handle this better than most by planning for it and making sure you stay on top of things.
- **VENUS IN CAPRICORN.** You might find yourself getting a little down in the dumps, as you're even harder on yourself than usual. Try a little self-care.
- **SATURN IN CAPRICORN.** You're naturally structured, and with Saturn hanging around, it gets to be a little too much. Give yourself some breaks, take it easy, and let loose!

Events to Look Forward To

- **MOON IN CAPRICORN.** The moon will make you a little more emotional than you like to be, but it will also help you really enjoy and connect with those you love.

- **SUN IN CAPRICORN.** Take this time to let loose and do things that are simply *fun*. Make it a full birthday month!

- **MERCURY IN CAPRICORN.** You're always pretty focused, and now even more so!

- **MARS IN CAPRICORN.** You'll reach completion on a number of projects during this time, as all your hard work pays off.

- **JUPITER IN CAPRICORN.** You'll be feeling more optimistic than usual now—take advantage of it and lean into your self-confidence.

Decans

SATURN DECAN
December 22–December 31

All Capricorns are driven, but you are even more so. You're very responsible and can seem overly serious, but the right people will spark your sense of humor.

- **ASPECTS TO CELEBRATE.** You are trustworthy and loyal. If something needs doing, consider it already done.

- **ASPECTS TO USE WITH CAUTION.** You sometimes have trouble taking breaks and thinking about what really makes you happy.
- **POTENTIAL CAREERS.** You could do literally anything you set your mind to, but you're likely drawn to work that allows you to manage the world around you. So either a CEO or the owner of your own business would work for you.

VENUS DECAN
January 1–January 10

You're a little gentler on yourself than other Capricorns and more able to bounce back from mistakes. You want to do well, but you're not quite as ambitious.

- **ASPECTS TO CELEBRATE.** You're really good at making the best of things. If there's trouble, you're always able to find the silver lining.
- **ASPECTS TO USE WITH CAUTION.** You do a lot for others, but have a hard time expressing yourself, particularly your deepest emotions.
- **POTENTIAL CAREERS.** You might consider working as a manager— you could handle a big team, keeping track of everything and making sure everyone has what they need. You'd also be a good financial advisor.

CAPRICORN

MERCURY DECAN
January 11–January 19

You have an easier time communicating your thoughts and feelings with others and allowing a little more flow. This lets you be more creative, though you are still extremely hardworking.

- **ASPECTS TO CELEBRATE.** You're often surprisingly funny, with a sarcastic sense of humor, and you never take yourself too seriously.

- **ASPECTS TO USE WiTH CAUTION.** You don't handle disappointment well. Try to remember that sometimes there simply isn't anything you could have done differently, and it just wasn't meant to be.

- **POTENTIAL CAREERS.** You'd be a great architect, or you could be a creative director of a theater or museum.

Aquarius

JANUARY 20–FEBRUARY 18

••••••

Y ou don't like labels or being told who you are. And no one could ever put you in a box because you are changeable— always reinventing yourself, evolving, and growing. You are always striving to be better, working to make yourself into the person you want to be.

You spend just as much time to make the world into the place you want it to be. You believe in social justice because you see how deeply interconnected we all are, and your sense of empathy helps you imagine what it's like to experience a life entirely different from your own. You're intelligent and use your mental powers for good. If you aren't sufficiently challenged, you can get bored, so watch that in school.

You can seem a little emotionally distant, particularly on an individual level—you are sometimes focused on the big picture and have trouble coming down to the everyday. This doesn't mean you don't care, but it can sometimes appear that way, so take care to let your friends and family know that you hear and see them.

You may—or may not, as you are very independent—be drawn to turquoise, violet, or yellow. Regardless, you look great in whatever you wear; your confidence gives you an individual style that always works for you.

Compatibility

- **FRIENDS WITH:** You get along well with Geminis, who will understand your changeable nature, and Sagittarians. You and other Aquariuses tend to understand each other, and while it may seem like a surprise given how opposite you are, you and Aries actually have a lot in common.
- **BEST FRIEND:** And yet the person you are likely to find yourself most at ease with is Libra. Their sense of balance will help you maintain your center, even at your most shape-shifting moments.

Famous Aquarius

BOB MARLEY
February 6, 1945–May 11, 1981

"Man is a universe within himself."

Bob Marley was born in a rural Jamaican village. Jamaica was still a colony of the British government at the time, and his father was a white official there. Children of mixed race were treated with scorn by both sides then, and things didn't get better when Marley and his mother moved to Kingston. They lived in Trench Town, a neighborhood made up of corrugated iron and tar paper shacks. But it was there that Marley found music.

Kingston's rhythm and blues scene was just starting to develop its own, unique sound, with distinctive offbeat. When Marley began writing his own music, he talked about his experiences, the poverty in Trench Town, and the racism that permeated Jamaica. And at the same time, he called for a peaceful protest, arguing against the gangs that had formed in Kingston.

Slowly, Marley's music became a sensation. This new sound, reggae, still represented his homeland and the truths he wanted to bring to light, but was appealing to listeners outside of Jamaica, as well. As he sang about the need for equality, both financial and racial, his songs soared in popularity and impact . . . and this angered the people in power in Jamaica. One night while he was rehearsing, he and his wife and manager were shot at and severely injured.

But this didn't stop Marley, and he continued to write and sing right up until his death, always asking for both justice and peace.

AQUARIUS CRAFT:

Soap

This glycerin soap will keep your skin smooth, retaining moisture while still getting squeaky clean, for a fresh start every day.

MATERIALS

- Scissors
- Clean milk or juice carton
- Petroleum jelly
- Block of melt and pour glycerin, available at most craft stores
- Chopstick for stirring
- Fragrance oil of your choice
- Food coloring
- Knife

Cut off the top of your milk or juice carton so you can pour the soap in more easily. Coat the inside of the carton with petroleum jelly to keep the soap from sticking.

Melt your glycerin according to the package instructions—you can put it in the microwave, checking and stirring every fifteen seconds. When it is fully melted, pour it into the milk carton.

Add your fragrance oil, two teaspoons for each pound of soap, and stir well. Add a few drops of food coloring and swirl them around with your chopstick. Now add a few drops of a similar food coloring—one that will enhance your first color if they end up blending a little (like green or purple if you started with blue or orange or yellow if you started with red), and swirl them as well, playing with your design. Don't overstir, or you'll just end up with soap that's just one color.

Let your soap cool for at least two hours, then pull apart the carton. Take a knife and slice your soap into bars.

Events to Watch Out For

- **MOON IN AQUARIUS.** You're always pretty kooky, but with the moon in your sign, things are going to be even wackier than usual. Hang on to your self-awareness.

- **MERCURY RETROGRADE.** You'll find yourself getting into little arguments and fights, as you misunderstand people and they misunderstand you. Make an extra effort to listen and explain.
- **MARS IN AQUARIUS.** You get an extra boost of confidence here—which is nice—but you also get more stubborn . . . and you're pretty stubborn already.

Events to Look Forward To

- **SUN IN AQUARIUS.** Plan something special with your friends, something you'll really enjoy—no matter how quirky it is!
- **MERCURY IN AQUARIUS.** Having Mercury around helps you stay more grounded and more able to communicate what's going on in your head.
- **VENUS IN AQUARIUS.** You and your friends get along really well during this time, just enjoying each other's company and having fun together. You feel really close to everyone and really comfortable with them.

- **JUPITER IN AQUARIUS.** You're bursting with big ideas and feeling in the flow.
- **SATURN IN AQUARIUS.** Saturn will give you more structure than you're used to, and it will serve you well.

Decans

URANUS DECAN
January 20–February 2

Some may see you as eccentric or weird, but you're just being you, completely and fully. You know who you want to be in the world, and you honestly don't care what others might think about that.

- **ASPECTS TO CELEBRATE.** You're quick-thinking and idealistic, and while you care about everyone, you are really close to only a small group of people—those you've chosen and truly love.
- **ASPECTS TO USE WITH CAUTION.** You have trouble committing to plans and schedules, because you really like to be free to do your own thing.
- **POTENTIAL CAREERS.** You could be a researcher for a think tank, working to come up with better ways to handle social issues like homelessness, medical care, etc.

MERCURY DECAN
February 3–February 12

All Aquariuses have big ideas, but you'll have an easier time expressing them and bringing others on board.

- **ASPECTS TO CELEBRATE.** You're spontaneous, childlike, and very honest.
- **ASPECTS TO USE WITH CAUTION.** You're quite restless and can sometimes think that when people are asking something of you, they're just hassling you. Consider whether that's really true.
- **POTENTIAL CAREERS.** You'll want to do something that allows you to make use of your big ideas—fundraising for a cause you believe in or teaching philosophy would be some good possibilities.

VENUS DECAN
February 13–February 18

You value your close relationships highly, and you think carefully about what others are going through. You are very fair and want the best for everyone.

- **ASPECTS TO CELEBRATE.** You are always around to offer advice, and it's *good* advice because you pay attention to what your friends really want, deep down.
- **ASPECTS TO USE WITH CAUTION.** You get bored easily and frustrated when other people aren't as lively as you are.
- **POTENTIAL CAREERS.** You'd be a fantastic judge or social worker.

Pisces

FEBRUARY 19–MARCH 20

•••••

You are friendly and love being surrounded by many different kinds of people. Like all Water Signs, you are naturally empathetic, and with Neptune as your ruling planet you have more intuition than most. You're a great friend and want to talk about everything, so you're the person people come to when they want to work something out.

You're also very artistic and drawn to creative pursuits of all kinds, especially music. You use your emotion and your intuition in your art, making it stand out and drawing the attention of others, as it resonates with them in a way they perhaps don't quite understand.

You have an internal wisdom that you trust, and your instincts are good. But you can sometimes be overly fearful, particularly of someone hurting your feelings. And when you do get hurt, you hold on to that hurt for a long time and struggle to get over it.

You're quite dreamy and can get lost in your own imagination. You're romantic and caring and are drawn to pinks and lilacs.

Compatibility

- **FRIENDS WITH:** You get along well with Scorpios and Cancers, as Water Signs tend to stick together. You also like the steadiness of a Taurus, though they don't always get you.
- **BEST FRIEND:** Practical Capricorn will help keep you grounded and will make you feel safe. You can always trust that they will be there for you.

Famous Pisces

RUTH BADER GINSBURG
March 15, 1933–September 18, 2020

*"I think daughters can change
the perceptions of their fathers."*

Ruth Bader Ginsburg was born in a working-class neighborhood in Brooklyn. Her mother died shortly before she graduated from high school, but was still one of the most profound influences on her life, teaching her the value of hard work, passion, and compromise. When Ginsburg attended Harvard Law, she was one of only eight women in her class and was already a wife and mother.

Despite her stellar academics, Supreme Court Justice Felix Frankfurter refused to hire her as a clerk because of her gender. Undeterred, Ginsburg spent her career advocating for gender equality and fighting for equal pay for equal work—something she herself did not receive when she taught at Rutgers. She was told that she would receive a lower salary because her husband also had an income.

In 1972, Ginsburg cofounded the Women's Rights Project at the American Civil Liberties Union, and the following year she became the project's general counsel. In her time there, she argued six cases before the Supreme Court and won five of them. Her dedication to true gender equality was sincere; one of those cases gave men the same benefits women received upon the death of a spouse.

She was appointed to the Supreme Court in 1993 and was only the second female justice. While she sat comfortably on the "liberal" wing of the Court, she strove to find common ground, ruling only when she felt there was a strong legal foundation regardless of her personal beliefs. She was a vocal dissenter, writing strong opinions when she disagreed with the Court's decision, but she maintained a friendly relationship even with those she found herself opposing.

PISCES CRAFT:
Body Scrub

This exfoliating scrub will moisturize your skin and make you smell and feel great. The sugar and coconut oil clear off the old and seal in the new.

MATERIALS

- ❖ ½ cup coconut oil
- ❖ Approximately 1 cup white sugar
- ❖ Red and blue food coloring
- ❖ Lavender essential oil
- ❖ Small glass jar

Heat the coconut oil in the microwave on low until it reaches a liquid state. Stir in your sugar, adding as much as you need to reach your desired consistency—you want it to feel pretty solid and not too oily and to look a bit like a snow cone.

Add a drop or two of red food coloring and a drop or two of blue until you reach a shade of lavender you like. Then stir in around ten drops of essential oil—a little goes a long way!

Scoop it into your glass jar and enjoy!

Events to Watch Out For

- **MOON IN PISCES.** You're fairly moody during this time, so try to pay attention to your emotional state to keep your center.

- **MERCURY RETROGRADE.** You're always a daydreamer, but now you'll get confused easily and have trouble concentrating. Try and maintain your focus as best you can.

- **VENUS IN PISCES.** You're even more emotional than usual and may get your feelings hurt more easily. Take care of yourself.

- **SATURN IN PISCES.** You'll feel a bit like the weight of the world is on your shoulders, as if you're responsible for everyone else's happiness. You're not.

Events to Look Forward To

- **SUN IN PISCES.** Throw yourself a fantastic party and have all your friends come. You love being surrounded by people—enjoy it!

- **MERCURY IN PISCES.** You are always open and communicative, and now you'll find yourself able to speak about the things that matter most to you—and everyone else will be right there with you.

- **MARS IN PISCES.** The fiery force of Mars will bring forward aspects of yourself you're not used to experiencing. You'll be more assertive, which is great!

- **JUPITER IN PISCES.** Your empathy is at its height, and you are so helpful to so many people at this time.

- **NEPTUNE IN PISCES.** Your intuition is off the charts, and your imagination is going crazy. This is definitely a good thing, but you need to remain tethered to the earth in order to put all those creative ideas to good use. You'll have Neptune inspiring you for fourteen years, so stay grounded.

Decans

NEPTUNE DECAN
February 19–March 3

You are so tuned in to others that it often seems like you can read their minds—or perhaps it's their hearts. You look out for everyone.

- **ASPECTS TO CELEBRATE.** You are always kind and thoughtful and expect the same of others.
- **ASPECTS TO USE WITH CAUTION.** You aren't very assertive and can sometimes expect people to guess what it is you want from them—make sure to tell them what you need!
- **POTENTIAL CAREERS.** You'd be the kind of teacher that could influence their students for generations. You would also be a great therapist, particularly for those who have suffered a trauma.

MOON DECAN
February 4–February 12

You are very funny and very passionate. You have strong emotions, but you manage them well, keeping balanced and happy.

- **ASPECTS TO CELEBRATE.** You love beauty, and you create it easily, using your imagination.
- **ASPECTS TO USE WITH CAUTION.** You sometimes have a hard time letting go of a friendship that isn't really working anymore.
- **POTENTIAL CAREERS.** You're a natural artist! You could use this in creating whatever strikes you, though you may well be a songwriter.

MARS DECAN
March 13–March 20

You are a visionary, and you dream big. You've got fantastic ideas for how to do just about anything from inventions to creating entire worlds.

- **ASPECTS TO CELEBRATE.** You can be impulsive, but you always bounce back, jumping onward to the next thing that excites you.
- **ASPECTS TO USE WITH CAUTION.** You sometimes have a hard time staying focused on following through on those big ideas. Stick with them!
- **POTENTIAL CAREERS.** You might be a science fiction writer, a fashion designer, or a game developer.

GLOSSARY

AIR SIGN. Signs that are ruled by the element of air and are therefore intellectual, good at communication, and thoughtful. The Air Signs are Aquarius, Gemini, and Libra.

ASTROLOGY. An ancient study of the planets and how they affect life on earth.

DECAN. One of three subsections of each sign, with small deviations from the usual characteristics of the sign.

EARTH SIGN. Signs that are ruled by the element of earth and are therefore dependable, organized, and pragmatic. The Earth Signs are Taurus, Virgo, and Capricorn.

FIRE SIGN. Signs that are ruled by the element of fire and are therefore passionate, temperamental, and creative. The Fire Signs are Aries, Leo, and Sagittarius.

JUPITER. The fifth planet from the sun and the ruler of growth, healing, and good fortune.

LUNAR ECLIPSE. When the moon moves into the earth's shadow.

MARS. The fourth planet from the sun and the ruler of confidence, energy, strength, and ambition.

MERCURY. The first planet from the sun and the ruler of communication, reasoning, and adaptability.

MERCURY RETROGRADE. When Mercury's orbit appears to be heading backward, reversing direction across the sky.